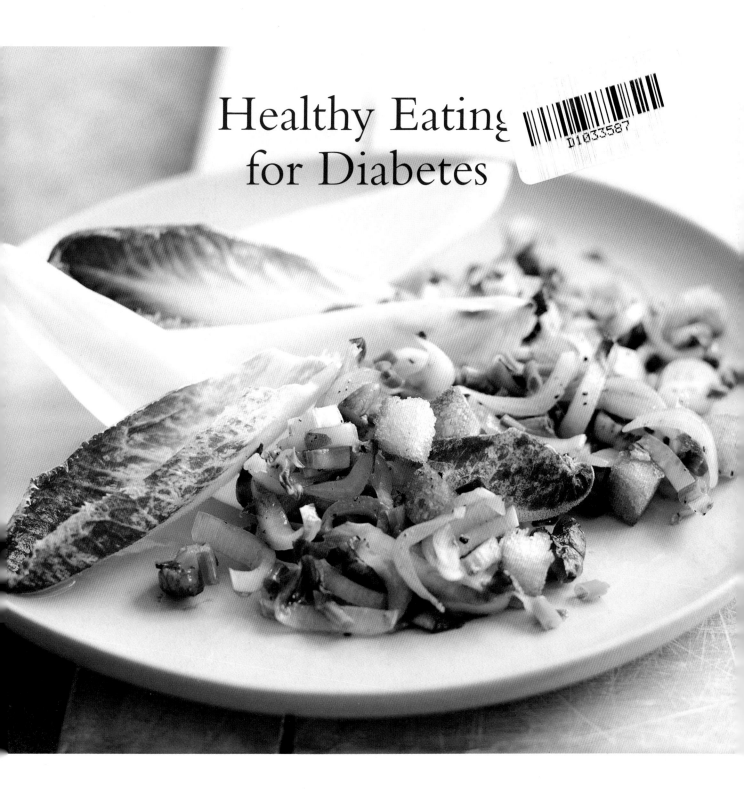

Healthy Eating
for Diabetes

Antony Worrall Thompson   Azmina Govindji BSc RD

Healthy
Eating
for
Diabetes

photography by Steve Lee

whitecap

Breakfasts and Brunches 39

Soups and Salads 49

Light Meals and Appetisers 75

Main Courses 99

Desserts 127

Dedication

To Frank Shiel, my new Dad and father in law, who was recently diagnosed with diabetes.

There are too many people to thank, but certain individuals deserve a special mention:
To my wonderful wife, Jacinta and our two children, Toby and Billie, who suffered from my lack of quality time yet supported me throughout as I managed to juggle my time through 3 books and everything else going on in my life.

To Louise, my energetic and ultra-efficient PA, who fielded hundreds of phone calls from the publishers and who was regularly on hand to smooth troubled waters when the pressures of deadlines occasionally took their toll.

To Fiona Lindsay, Linda Shanks and Lesley Turnbull at Limelight Management, who are constantly there to make sure I have more than enough work to handle.

To my team at Notting Grill, especially David, George and Candido, who kept the boat afloat in my often extended absences.

To the various friends Nicki, Kate, Sarah, Margot, Suzie, June, Anne and John, and Mike and Nicky who acted unknowingly as guinea pigs for many of the recipes.

To Azmina Govindji, who waited patiently for the recipes so that she could nutritionally analyse them and for producing an excellent section on the whys and wherefores of diabetes, much of which I had limited knowledge of.

And finally to Muna Reyal, my editor and her fab team at Kyle Cathie for giving me the opportunity to produce this cook book. They turned my offerings into a beautifully executed book that people with diabetes will find easy to understand and hopefully they will realise life doesn't have to change that much when it comes to eating.

Important note

The information and advice contained in this book are intended as a general guide to healthy eating and are not specific to individuals or their particular circumstances. This book is not intended to replace treatment by a qualified practitioner. Neither the authors nor the publishers can be held responsible for claims arising from the inappropriate use of any dietary regime. Do not attempt self-diagnosis or self-treatment for serious or long-term conditions without consulting a medical professional or qualified practitioner.

For too many years, people with diabetes have seen their diagnosis as marking the end of enjoyable meals and the beginning of a poorer quality of life. Today, with fresh ingredients and the influences of international cuisine, this is no longer true, as Antony and Azmina have proved so clearly in this wonderful book. Dispelling the myth that the diabetic diet is dull, while also improving understanding of diabetes and nutrition, *Healthy Eating for Diabetes* is both educational and inspiring. We are delighted to support this collaboration and encourage anyone with diabetes looking to improve their well-being as well as their diet to add this book to their collection.

The Diabetes Research & Wellness Foundation (DRWF) is a registered national charity, established to raise money for research into diabetes, while supporting people living with the condition and raising public awareness. Through our Diabetes Wellness Network we provide professional support, information and advice, as well as news of the latest research developments at home and abroad.

Promoting wellness and a better quality of life is central to our work at DRWF. We recognise that, for many people, improved understanding can be the key to successful management of this chronic condition. Each month our newsletter, *Diabetes Wellness News*, includes articles on diabetes healthcare, answers to specific health questions and enlightening, and often inspiring, personal stories. This newsletter is an essential tool in keeping abreast of the latest professional advice and getting to grips with diabetes.

Specially tailored events are also run to help improve self-management and encourage learning from both healthcare professionals and other people living with diabetes. Our Wellness Weekends and Retreats, as well as Active with Diabetes holidays, are held each year for anyone seeking advice, reassurance or the opportunity to be active in the company of other people with diabetes.

At DRWF we welcome new members who want to become part of a Network of people with diabetes, their families and friends. We also welcome donations to help us finance further research into diabetes in institutions across the UK.

For more information or to subscribe to the Diabetes Wellness Network, please write to us at: 101–102, Northney Marina, Hayling Is. Hampshire PO11 0NH or telephone 023 9263 7808.

James A. S. Rogers LL.B.
Executive Director, Diabetes Research & Wellness Foundation

What Is Diabetes?

Have you been newly diagnosed with diabetes? Or does someone in the family have diabetes? If so, read on for some home truths on just what diabetes is and how to live with it and still enjoy a full and active life.

When you have diabetes, the amount of glucose (sugar) in your blood is too high because your body is unable to use it properly. A hormone called insulin helps glucose to enter the cells where it is used as fuel by your body. If there is not enough insulin, or if the insulin you have is not working properly, then glucose can build up in your blood as a result.

Types of diabetes

- Type 1 or insulin-dependent diabetes occurs when there is a severe lack of insulin in the body. It is treated by insulin injections and a healthy range of foods.
- Type 2 or non-insulin-dependent diabetes is the most common type and over 80 per cent of people who have it are overweight. In type 2 diabetes the body can still make some insulin, but not enough for its needs. It can be treated by a healthy diet alone, or by diet and tablets, or sometimes by diet and insulin injections.

What causes diabetes?

There is no one cause of diabetes and it seems to be caused by a combination of genetic and environmental factors. We know that it runs in families and we also know that if you are overweight you are more likely to get type 2 diabetes.

There is no cure for diabetes yet, and there is no such thing as mild diabetes. The main aim of treatment is to avoid 'highs' and 'lows' in your blood glucose level. Together with a healthy lifestyle, this will help to improve your well-being and protect against long-term damage to your eyes, kidneys, nerves and heart.

Knowing the tell-tale signs

One of the difficulties with diabetes is that you might actually be symptom-free (particularly if you have type 2). Many people are diagnosed only after a routine examination by their GP. So, if you think you may have diabetes (for example, if you have a family history or one or more of the risk factors below), a simple blood test can put your mind at ease. Spotting the condition early will mean that it can be treated.

What to look out for

If you notice any of the following it could be an indication that you have diabetes:

- increased thirst, especially for sweet drinks
- you go to the toilet a lot, especially at night
- you feel very tired
- you are losing weight unexpectedly
- itching of the genital organs or recurrent thrush
- blurred vision.

The above symptoms are characteristic of type 1 diabetes, which is easier to diagnose and the symptoms can be quickly relieved with treatment. However, if you have type 2 diabetes, which is more common in people over forty, these symptoms may be less apparent or even non-existent.

Low blood sugar

The medical term for low blood sugar is 'hypoglycaemia', although it is more commonly referred to as a 'hypo'. This is generally speaking most likely to occur in people treated with insulin. It can be caused by:

- missing a meal or snack
- engaging in strenuous activity without enough food beforehand
- injecting more insulin than is needed
- drinking alcohol on an empty stomach.

Sometimes, however, there may be no obvious reason for a hypo. Signs and symptoms of a hypo vary, but the common ones are light-headedness, a faint feeling, sweating, shaking, hunger and confusion.

A hypo should be treated by taking a dextrose tablet, sugared water or a sugar lump immediately to raise your blood sugar quickly, followed by (within half an hour) something more substantial (such as a glass of milk and a slice of toast) to maintain a good blood sugar level.

Syndrome X

You may have heard about the term Syndrome X and wondered what it was. It sounds like something from a science-fiction movie but it actually refers to a collection of medical conditions. These include:

- central obesity, which means a waist measurement of more than 94cm (37in) for men (92cm/36in for South Asian men as they have been found to be even more at risk) and more than 82cm (32in) in women
- poor blood sugar control
- high blood pressure
- abnormal blood fats including raised triglycerides and low HDL (the 'good' form of cholesterol – see page 16)
- 'sticky blood' with an increased tendency to form clots.

A diagnosis of Syndrome X is reached when three or more of these conditions occur together. Each of them is an independent risk factor for heart disease and having more than one increases the risk considerably.

What causes it?

Syndrome X is also sometimes referred to as 'metabolic syndrome' or 'insulin resistance syndrome'. There appears to be a genetic factor at work, so having a family member with Syndrome X increases your risk. Current thinking is that all the conditions associated with it arise from one main cause: insulin resistance (IR). IR is a reduced sensitivity in the tissues of the body to the action of circulating insulin. As a result, the pancreas reacts by trying to produce more insulin, leading to high circulating levels in the blood. If the insulin resistance becomes severe, type 2 diabetes can develop.

How common is it?

Syndrome X seems to be very common in the Western world. Estimates from the USA and Scandinavia suggest that between 10 and 25 per cent of adults show some degree of insulin resistance. Syndrome X is sometimes said to be 'silent' since most people who have it are unaware of it.

Risk factors include obesity, a family history of type 2 diabetes and a history of diabetes during pregnancy.

What can you do if you have Syndrome X?

Research has shown that both insulin resistance and the symptoms of Syndrome X can be improved by lifestyle changes, including physical activity and healthy eating. There is some research to suggest that a diet based mainly on foods with a low glycaemic index (see page 12) may improve insulin sensitivity in people with type 2 diabetes, but their role in Syndrome X is not clear at present. The good news is that these approaches, if successfully adopted, are very effective in reducing the risk of heart disease and of developing type 2 diabetes.

Lifestyle Guidelines for Syndrome X

- Take regular physical exercise – activities such as brisk walking.
- Cut down on the amount of fat and especially saturated fat in your diet. Replace this with mono and polyunsaturated fats from vegetable sources and fish.
- Choose starchy carbohydrate and fibre-rich foods, fruit and vegetables.
- Keep your body weight to within 20 per cent of ideal targets.
- Drink alcohol in moderation only.
- Don't smoke.

Food Facts

What you eat is the most important part of your diabetes treatment. Whether you need to take medication or not, the foods you choose and how often you eat have a significant impact on your blood glucose. What you eat also affects the amount of fat (like cholesterol) in your blood. If you have diabetes, you already have an increased risk of developing heart disease, so watching what you eat is particularly important. Insulin or tablets are not a substitute for a healthy diet.

There are lots of healthy eating tips in this book. It's a good idea to pick out the changes that you feel will easily fit into your lifestyle, choosing foods you enjoy. Don't think in terms of foods that you must or must not eat. Healthy eating is all about balance – selecting a variety of healthy foods you enjoy and not forcing yourself to eat foods you dislike.

A taste of the Mediterranean

The Mediterranean way of eating, with its abundance of olive oil, garlic, fish, nuts, fruit and vegetables, has been associated with a lower risk of conditions such as coronary heart disease and cancer, so incorporating foods from Mediterranean cuisine into the diet for diabetes makes sense. And the good news is that recent research supports the idea that eating the right types of fat may be more important than making your fat intake really low. It has been shown that the total amount of fat eaten by people who live in Mediterranean countries is actually quite high, but when you take a closer look, you see that it's high in monounsaturated oils (such as olive oil), and omega-3 fats (such as those found in oily fish).

Research suggests that even as little as 25g (1oz) of oily fish (such as salmon, herring, mackerel and tuna) a day can significantly reduce the incidence of heart disease, and it even benefits those people who have already suffered a heart attack. People in Mediterranean countries also eat more fruit and vegetables, so they benefit from a good antioxidant intake (see page 22), as well as more garlic and the classic glass of red wine, both of which have been shown to have therapeutic properties. Garlic has been shown to thin the blood, helping it to flow more smoothly, whilst the active ingredients in red wine, phenols, act in a similar way to the antioxidant vitamins, so that one glass a day is thought to be protective against heart disease.

Starchy foods

Starchy carbohydrate foods (such as bread, rice, pasta, cereals, chapatis and potatoes) are healthy and naturally low in fat. Many recipes is this book contain pasta, which is an excellent starchy food for people with diabetes. Starchy foods are also filling, and if they are cooked properly in minimal fat, they can be helpful if you are trying to lose weight.

Wholegrain varieties of bread and cereals as well as the skin on potatoes are high in fibre. High-fibre starchy foods such as bran-based cereals and wholemeal bread are especially useful in preventing constipation. A high-fibre diet is good for the whole family, but remember that when you eat more fibre, it is important to drink more fluid. Try to drink at least six to eight cups of fluid each day.

Oat-based cereals like porridge and muesli are high in soluble fibre. These foods are often more slowly absorbed than starchy foods in general and they can play a significant part in keeping your blood glucose within a healthy range. Instant hot oat cereals do contain soluble fibre, but because the oats have been 'mashed up' they have less effect on slowing down the rise in blood glucose after meals.

It is important to spread your intake of starchy foods evenly through the day and to eat regular meals. This helps to reduce fluctuations in your blood glucose levels.

Carbohydrates

Flicking through a newspaper it is neither unusual nor surprising to see many articles on the latest trend in carbohydrates, whether they are telling you to 'avoid wheat', that 'starchy foods are fattening', or that 'pasta is the best food ever invented'. How are you to know what's best in the case of diabetes? And is all this conflicting advice, or do the experts agree? Let's review some of the more confusing issues here.

The chemical structure of carbohydrates affects how they are metabolised. Simple carbs are made up of shorter chains of sugar, while complex carbs are made up of longer structures.

SUGAR ('SIMPLE' CARBOHYDRATES)	STARCHES ('COMPLEX' CARBOHYDRATES)
Glucose	Breads, including chapatis, pitta
Fructose, found in fruit, some vegetables and honey	Tortillas, etc.
	Pasta, noodles
Sucrose, as in tabletop sugar	Rice
	Potatoes, plantains, cassava, yams
Maltose	
Lactose, found only in milk and milk products	Cereals

The low-carb way of eating

Low-carb diets, perhaps the best-known example of which is the Atkins diet, typically involve basing meals on meat, poultry, fish, eggs and cheese, whilst severely restricting all carbohydrate-rich foods such as bread, potatoes, pasta, rice, pizza, crisps, cereals and sugars. They also limit most fruits, some vegetables and many alcoholic drinks.

Some of these diets allow large amounts of butter, oil, cheese and fatty meats, but such diets tend to be high in protein. Too much protein can place a strain on the kidneys, and since people with diabetes may be at risk of developing kidney problems, a high intake may be harmful. Whilst more carbohydrate is allowed when you are trying to maintain the weight loss, the overall diet actually conflicts with the current international consensus for both good health and weight control. There really is not, at present, scientific evidence to support the need to go to such low-carb extremes, especially for someone with diabetes.

Are carbs acceptable?

So, is pasta in or out? Should you be giving potatoes a miss? Meals are best tailored to the individual, rather than everyone aiming for the same goals, as some people will do better on less starchy foods than others.

Most people with type 2 diabetes would benefit from losing weight, so filling up on starchy foods which add calories is unhelpful. If balanced meals and snacks are maintained, there's no reason why favourite starchy foods cannot be a part of the daily food intake. In fact, there are some carbohydrates that are actively encouraged – those with a low glycaemic index (GI; see below).

When it comes to sugar, which is also a carbohydrate food, the advice is different, but again, forget the myth that you can't have any sweet tastes in diabetes – see page 15 for more on sugar.

Glycaemic index (GI)

When you eat carbohydrate foods (such as bread, potatoes, pasta or cereals), the body digests the starch until, eventually, it becomes glucose (sugar). This can then be used by the body for energy and it is this glucose which contributes to the glucose levels in your blood.

Glucose also comes from other foods, but mainly from the starchy and sugary foods. So, is it as simple as just watching the starch and sugar in your diet? New research shows that not all carbohydrate foods have the same effect on blood glucose. Furthermore, the amount and type of fat, the type of fibre and even the way food are cooked is more important.

The GI is a ranking of foods relating to how these foods affect blood glucose levels. The faster a food is broken down during digestion, the quicker will be the rise in blood glucose. Since one of the main aims of treatment of diabetes is to keep blood glucose levels steady throughout the day, foods which cause sharp rises are best kept to a minimum, except in special circumstances, such as illness, hypoglycaemia (see page 8) or exercise. Foods that cause a rapid rise in blood glucose will have a high GI, so the key is to choose more low-GI foods regularly (see pages 13 and 14). The effect of a low-GI meal can run into the following meal, which helps to keep blood glucose more even throughout the day.

Since low-GI foods reduce the peaks in blood glucose that often follow a meal, they may have a role in helping to prevent or reduce the risk of getting type 2 diabetes if you are at risk, as in Syndrome X (see page 9). Low-GI foods can help you to eat less as you feel fuller for longer. Research has also shown that people who follow an overall low-GI diet have a lower incidence of heart disease and lower-GI diets have also been associated with improved levels of 'good' cholesterol (see page 16).

Which foods should you go for?

'Whole' foods, such as wholegrains, and those high in soluble fibre, for example kidney beans, will take longer to be broken down by the body and will thus cause a slower rise in blood glucose. If you imagine how easy it is to digest puréed pea soup which is already in small particles, it would make sense to suggest that the body doesn't need to mash this up for too long before it is ready to enter the bloodstream as glucose. Now imagine how much longer it would take to digest whole peas. The body needs to break down the skin of the peas before it even reaches the pulp, then it needs to break that down into a mush before it is small enough to enter the bloodstream. Whole peas will therefore make the blood glucose rise more slowly than the puréed soup. This is the case with most foods. Compare hummus to a whole chickpea casserole, mashed potatoes to a jacket potato and seeded bread to wholemeal.

Look at the whole food

It's important to know that not all low- or medium-GI foods are recommended for good health. The addition of fat and protein, for example, slows down the absorption of carbohydrate, giving foods a lower GI, so that chocolate, for instance, has a medium GI because of its

fat content. And crisps and chips actually have a lower GI than potatoes cooked without fat. Milk and other dairy products have a low GI because of their high protein content, and the fact that they contain fat. So, if you choose only low-GI foods, your diet could be unbalanced and high in fat, which could lead to weight gain and an increased risk of heart disease. Overall balance is, then, the key to healthy eating and the right mix of foods will not only ensure better

control of your blood glucose, but will also help you to obtain the wide variety of nutrients needed for good health.

The table on page 15 gives a comparison of the GI levels of various foods. The GI of a food only tells you how quickly or slowly it raises the blood glucose when the food is eaten on its own, so you need to bear in mind that in practice we generally eat foods in combination: bread is usually eaten with butter or margarine; potatoes are often

LOW-GI FOODS	MEDIUM-GI FOODS	HIGH-GI FOODS
Muesli and porridge	Beetroot	Bagels
Multi-grain and rye bread	Basmati rice	White & wholemeal bread
Fruit loaf	Potatoes, boiled	Water biscuits
Pasta	Rich tea biscuits	Glucose drinks
Baked beans	Pitta bread	Corn chips (tortilla crisps)
Lentils	Wheat biscuits (e.g.	Corn flakes
Apples, oranges and pears	(Weetabix)	Puffed wheat
Yogurt	Couscous	Puffed rice
Sweetcorn	Ice cream	Sugar-rich breakfast cereals
Bran cereals (e.g. All Bran,	Digestive biscuits	Sports drinks
Sultana Bran)	Honey	Waffles

eaten with meat and vegetables, etc. So cutting out all high-GI foods is not the answer; instead include more low-GI foods to lower the overall GI of meals.

The truth about sugar

Sugar is just calories; it has no benefits in terms of vitamins, minerals, protein or any other nutrient. However, we cannot ignore the fact that sugary foods taste good! So, whether you have diabetes or not, the advice is simple: enjoy a range of foods, focusing mainly on fruit, vegetables and starchy foods and limiting the amount of fatty and sugary foods you eat: you need not avoid them altogether.

In the past, it was believed that sugary foods automatically caused a rise in blood sugar and it therefore seemed to make sense to avoid these foods if you had diabetes. However, we now know that the effect of a particular food on blood sugar depends not only on how much sugar it contains, but also on a range of other factors including the way in which it is cooked, how it is served (i.e. whole, mashed or in between) and what else is eaten with it.

A drink which is high in sugar, for example, when taken on an empty stomach or in between meals, will cause a quick rise in blood glucose because it is rapidly absorbed into the bloodstream. However, if it is taken mixed with food, especially at the end of a high-fibre meal, the rise will take place more slowly. This is especially true if your meal contains foods with a low glycaemic index (see page 12). So, in short, small amounts of sugar are fine for people with diabetes if taken as part of an overall healthy eating plan and ideally at the end of a meal.

Desserts

Having diabetes does not mean saying goodbye to desserts. All sorts of sweets and puddings can be incorporated into your diet, particularly if you choose appropriate ingredients. Half-fat creams, low-fat instant dessert mixes, fresh and dried fruit can all help to reduce the fat and sugar content of traditional puddings. To make your desserts even lower in fat, try using virtually fat-free fromage frais or low-fat natural yogurt. Base desserts on fruit as often as possible and try to eat two to three fruits a day.

Sweeteners

Artificial sweeteners made from aspartame, saccharin and acesulfame potassium are sugar-free and will not cause a rise in your blood glucose levels. They may be used to sweeten foods but it is generally best to add them after cooking or in recipes that don't need to be heated as they sometimes develop a bitter aftertaste when heated to high temperatures. They are not, however, a good substitute for sugar in baking. Again, it's all a matter of personal choice. If you prefer to use an artificial sweetener (which, incidentally, is also calorie-free), then you can choose to do so, for example, in cereals and desserts. This will give you a food which in the end is lower in sugar and calories than if you'd used sugar. However, if you prefer to use a little sugar, ensure that the other foods in your meal are healthy by including, for instance, high-fibre cereal (such as porridge) for breakfast, beans and pulses in your main meals and fruit as the basis of desserts.

Fats

Advice given about fats can often sound confusing. If fats are so bad for you, how come some are essential? If spreading fats are better than hard fats like butter, why the caution with 'trans' fats in margarine? If a high blood cholesterol is unhealthy, how is it that foods which are high in cholesterol are not necessarily bad for you?

One of the key tips for eating well, whether you have diabetes or not, is to cut down on your fat intake. Saturated fat has been shown to raise a type of fat in your blood called cholesterol. A high blood cholesterol makes you more prone to heart problems. Since people with diabetes are at an increased risk of getting heart disease, watching your fat intake is particularly important.

The science behind cholesterol

Blood is delivered to the heart via the coronary arteries. As you get older, it is normal for these arteries to narrow, primarily as a result of Western lifestyle and food habits, which cause fatty deposits (atheroma) to be laid down within the artery walls. The fat then hardens (atherosclerosis), resulting in the reduction of the rate of blood flow. Also, it is likely that the hardened fat becomes damaged and blood cells form a clot as a means of protection. A large clot can block the artery completely, causing a heart attack. If your blood cholesterol is high, you are more likely to develop atherosclerosis.

Fat is transported around the blood as lipids, which are carried in tiny particles called lipoproteins. Although having high blood cholesterol increases your chances of having a heart attack, some blood cholesterol is not harmful at all. Often termed 'good' cholesterol, high-density lipoprotein (HDL) represents the cholesterol which is being taken away from the body tissues back to the liver. Most of your cholesterol is, however, carried in the low-density lipoprotein (LDL) or 'bad' cholesterol. A high LDL level can increase your risk of a heart attack as it leads to the formation of fatty deposits in the arteries.

Therefore, the higher your HDL, the lower your risk of heart disease.

Get your fats straight

Fats differ according to their chemical make-up. Saturated fats are associated

Did you know?

▶ Fat, weight for weight, provides twice the calories of starch or protein.

▶ Foods high in fat tend to be high in calories and are often also high in sugar.

▶ Essential fats are needed regularly in small amounts because they cannot be manufactured from other foods nor from within the body. Omega-3 and omega-6 fats – the essential fatty acids – are crucial for normal growth and development.

▶ Cutting down on fatty foods is the fastest way to reduce your calorie intake but if you go too low you may get bored and drive yourself into an eating frenzy!

▶ Fat acts as an important carrier for fat-soluble vitamins (A, D, E and K) in the bloodstream.

▶ Your liver produces cholesterol irrespective of the cholesterol in your diet.

▶ Cholesterol in food has less effect on your blood cholesterol than animal (saturated) fats.

▶ The ratio of fats in your diet as well as the quality has been shown to be beneficial to overall health (see above, 'Get your fats straight').

with raised blood cholesterol, and so it makes sense to keep a watchful eye on them. You do need some, but experts such as the Department of Health's Food Standards Agency recommend that no more than 10 per cent of your daily calorie intake should come from this group. The rest of your fat intake should come from monounsaturated and polyunsaturated fats.

Put simply:
- ▸ Saturated fats raise 'good' and 'bad' blood cholesterol (see page 16). They can also make the blood more 'sticky', making it more likely to clot. So cut down on these fats.
- ▸ Polyunsaturated fats appear to lower both 'good' and 'bad' blood cholesterol. Omega-3 and omega-6 fats are essential fatty acids that belong to this group. Omega-3s are the ones we should make a more conscious effort to eat more of, as we already get plenty of omega-6s from margarines and spreads.
- ▸ Monounsaturated fats lower 'bad' cholesterol and are thought to raise 'good' blood cholesterol. They are therefore recommended in preference to polyunsaturated fats. Hence, these are your best friends.
- ▸ Trans fats are usually by-products of hydrogenation, a process used to make unsaturated fats firm and spreadable. Research has shown that, like saturates, they raise blood cholesterol. Trans fats are found in

FATS	SOURCES	RECOMMENDATIONS
Monounsaturates	Olive oil, rapeseed oil groundnut oil, spreads made from these oils	Replace saturated fats with these wherever possible
Omega-3 polyunsaturated fats	Fish oils, rapeseed oil, olive oil, spreads made from fish oils, linseeds, soya beans	Eat more. Choose one portion of oily fish a week
Omega-6 polyunsaturated fats	Soya margarines, sunflower spreads, sunflower, soya bean, safflower, corn and grapeseed oils	Replace saturates with these, but eat in moderation
Trans fats	Hydrogenated spreads, processed foods made with trans fats	Keep to a minimum, remove from diet where possible
Saturates	Butter, lard, animal suet, processed foods made with saturates, fatty meat, skin on poultry	Cut down
Cholesterol	Eggs, shellfish, offal	Eat in sensible amounts as part of an overall low-fat diet

processed foods like biscuits, cakes and pastries (check the packets).
- ▸ Dietary cholesterol has little effect on blood cholesterol (see 'Did you know', page 16). A low-fat diet will generally also be low in cholesterol, so you need not be overly conscious of cholesterol levels in food (unless you have a blood disorder, which specifically requires dietary cholesterol modification).

Reducing fats
Use cooking-oil sprays, which are often a mixture of oil and water (make your own using 1 part oil to 7 parts water, or use a drizzle of olive or rapeseed oil), or a small amount of butter in cooking. Try reduced-fat dairy products, such as semi-skimmed or skimmed milk, half-fat cheese and low-fat yogurt. Base salad dressings on low-fat natural yogurt and lemon juice, or buy fat-free dressings.

Protein

The majority of people in the Western world eat more than enough protein and deficiency is extremely rare. Some surveys suggest that in the UK we get at least 50 per cent more protein than we need because of our ever-increasing portion sizes, especially of meat and dairy products. Too much protein can place a strain on and damage the kidneys, as they struggle to get rid of the excess. People with diabetes may be at higher risk of developing kidney problems (nephropathy) and are therefore advised to keep to sensible amounts and avoid higher-than-average intakes. This is especially important if you also have high blood pressure, which could increase the potential for damage.

If you already have kidney damage, you may be advised to limit protein intake more strictly and the specialist advice of a registered dietitian will be necessary.

Which protein foods are best?

There are vegetable (e.g. beans, pulses, nuts) and animal (e.g. meat, dairy products) sources of protein. Other than in the case of lean meat, fish and low-fat dairy products, animal sources do tend to be higher in saturated fat. Studies have found lower blood cholesterol and blood pressure and better blood-sugar control in people with diabetes who follow predominantly plant protein-based diets rather than in those who follow animal-based ones. This doesn't mean you should become a vegetarian. Simply vary your meals so that you include a good range of vegetarian foods often.

All proteins are made up from building blocks called amino acids, some of which are essential to the body. Vegetable proteins tend to be lacking in one or more essential amino acids but if you mix them together, you can achieve the right balance. Many vegetarian dishes are based on this principle. The table (left) offers tips on how to combine vegetable protein foods to get the best mix.

Mixing vegetable proteins

COMBINED FOOD GROUP	FOODS	EXAMPLE DISH
Cereals and pulses	Wheat and beans	Baked beans on toast Bruschetta with white bean purée and raw mushrooms (page 78)
	Rice and kidney beans	Jamaican rice and peas Vegetable chilli
	Rice or noodles and soya beans	Tofu stir-fry
	Wheat and lentils	Lentil soup and bread
	Rice and lentils	Dhal curry and rice
	Sweetcorn and beans	Tortilla and refried beans
Cereals and nuts	Wheat and peanuts	Peanut butter sandwich
	Wheat and nuts	Nut roast with breadcrumbs Chicory salad with walnuts and croûtons (page 65)
Pulses and seeds	Chickpeas and sesame seed paste	Hummus

Fruit and vegetables

These foods contain important vitamins that are needed for health, whether you have diabetes or not. A diet that contains plenty of fruit and vegetables will provide more fibre, especially the soluble variety, and more antioxidant vitamins and will usually be lower in fat. The antioxidant vitamins, beta-carotene (which is converted to vitamin A in the body), vitamins E and C, have been linked to a lower incidence of heart disease, some cancers and gut problems.

It is recommended that you eat five portions daily. Try to choose fruit and vegetables of varying colours, cook them quickly and serve them as whole as possible rather than puréed.

How much is enough?

For good health, you should aim for 400g (14oz), or about five 80g (3oz) portions per day. Potatoes are classified as starchy carbohydrates, so they don't count.

What constitutes a portion?

- Medium apple, pear, orange, banana
- Large slice of melon or pineapple
- Cupful of strawberries or grapes
- ½–1 tablespoon of dried fruit
- 1 small glass of fresh fruit juice
- 2 tablespoons of cooked vegetables
- Small serving of salad vegetables, e.g. a carrot, a tomato, or a small bowl of mixed salad
- 2 tablespoons of tinned vegetables, e.g. sweetcorn, baked beans

What about juice and dried fruit?

As you can see from the list, dried fruit and fresh fruit juice do count. However, it is best to choose juice as only one of your five portions, since the valuable fibre has been removed.

From the diabetes point of view, drinking large amounts of fruit juice, even if this is unsweetened, may make your blood glucose rise sharply. This is because the natural sugar in a liquid form is rapidly absorbed by the body. If you like fresh fruit juice, take it with a meal rather than on its own. Alternatively, choose a sugar-free squash or diet drink.

Pulses, such as beans and lentils, are good because they are high in soluble fibre which helps to control blood glucose levels (see page 13), but they can only be counted as one portion a day. This is because they don't contain the range of nutrients you get from other sources such as green leafy vegetables, carrots and tomatoes.

Antioxidants

These much-praised substances are found naturally in fruit and vegetables. They include vital vitamins such as vitamin A, C and E as well as lycopene (concentrated in tomatoes), flavanoids (found in tea) and selenium.

Antioxidants are thought to be protective since they 'mop up' free radicals, which are present in the body but can cause some of the problems associated with heart disease and cancer.

Free radicals are by-products of normal body processes but cigarette smoke, ultraviolet light, illness and pollution increase their production.

And lycopene, which is concentrated in tomatoes, becomes more potent when the tomatoes are processed. So smothering pasta with a jar of tomato-based pasta sauce might be cheating from the culinary point of view, but will ensure that your meal is packed with hidden benefits.

Do supplements do the trick?

The brightly coloured red, yellow and orange vegetables are particularly rich in antioxidants, especially beta-carotene. Packed with cancer-fighting power, these phyto-chemicals are present in fresh fruit and vegetables in precisely the quantities and combination Mother Nature intended. So taking a supplement with one or two of them just won't do the same job as the real foods themselves.

Meat, fish, nuts, pulses and eggs

These foods are rich in protein and many are good sources of vitamins and minerals, such as iron and zinc. However, meat can be high in saturated fat, so it is best to choose lean cuts and to minimise the oil you use in cooking. See 'Reducing fats' on page 17 for advice on lower-fat choices.

Meat dishes can be made healthier by adding beans or vegetables. This adds fibre, makes the meal go further and generally provides fewer calories per plate.

Salt and hypertension

High blood pressure makes you more prone to heart conditions. Since eating too much salt is linked with high blood pressure, cutting down may be protective. Salt is the common name for sodium chloride and it is the sodium part of salt which is harmful if taken in excess. It's estimated that people in the UK eat at least 10 grams or 2 teaspoons of salt each day. Most of the salt comes from manufactured foods, and it is very likely that you are taking in far more than this amount each day, especially if you rely heavily on processed meals and snacks. For good health, it is recommended that you keep your total daily salt intake (including that in manufactured foods) to 6 grams, or just over 1 teaspoon. This is equivalent to 2.5g of sodium.

Salt sense

- ▶ Measure the amount of salt you add in cooking and gradually cut down till a recipe that serves four people contains around ½ teaspoon of salt.
- ▶ Avoid adding salt at the table.
- ▶ Experiment with herbs and spices, using, for example, freshly ground spices, dried and fresh herbs, paprika and freshly milled black pepper. If you find it hard to get used to a less salty flavour, you can try a salt substitute. Low-salt products (such as vegetables canned in water, unsalted butter) can be used as replacements.
- ▶ For varied flavours, try lime juice, balsamic vinegar and chilli sauce.
- ▶ Read food labels carefully. Salt may appear as sodium, sodium chloride, monosodium glutamate or bicarbonate of soda. Multiply the sodium figure by 2.5 to find the salt content.
- ▶ Cut down on salty foods such as salted crisps, nuts, savoury biscuits and pastries.
- ▶ Salted and smoked foods such as bacon, sausages, smoked fish, some canned fish and other processed foods are often loaded with salt. Whenever possible, use fresh foods such as fish, lean meat, fruit and fresh vegetables. They have only a small amount of salt.

Salt substitutes

If you need to cut down on salt, you will find that in time your taste buds adjust and you will begin to prefer the taste of less salty foods. If you are still craving a salty flavour, however, a salt substitute is a practical and convenient way of reducing your salt intake. Read the label – some leading brands offer up to two thirds less sodium than ordinary salt, and you can use them in cooking and at the table. They are not recommended for people with kidney problems, however, as they contain potassium which can have a harmful effect on diseased kidneys.

Alcohol

If you have diabetes there's no reason why you shouldn't enjoy a drink, unless, of course, you have been advised to avoid alcohol for another medical reason.

Observe the safe drinking limit for everyone: between 21 and 28 units a week for men (or 3–4 units a day) and between 14 and 21 units a week for women (or 2–3 units a day). Note that these are the maximum recommended amounts and drinking less is preferable. Try to space your drinking throughout the week and to have two or three alcohol-free days each week.

Safe drinking

Alcohol can cause hypoglycaemia (a 'hypo', or low blood glucose, see page 8) if you are taking insulin or certain tablets for your diabetes, and the higher the alcohol content (such as in spirits), the more likely it is to cause a hypo. Here are some guidelines which may help to prevent this:

- ▶ Avoid drinking on an empty stomach. Always have something to eat with a drink and especially afterwards if you have been out drinking. This is because the hypoglycaemic effect of alcohol can last for several hours.
- ▶ Choose low-alcohol drinks; avoid special diabetic beers or lagers, as these are higher in alcohol.
- ▶ If you enjoy spirits, try to use the sugar-free/slimline mixers.
- ▶ If you count the amount of carbohydrate you eat, don't include the carbs from alcoholic drinks.
- ▶ Drink less if you are trying to lose weight and consume no more than 7 units of alcohol per week.

1 unit of alcohol is equal to:

- ▶ 300ml/½ pint beer or lager

- ▶ 1 pub measure of sherry, aperitif or liqueur (50ml/2fl oz)

- ▶ 1 standard glass of wine (125ml/4fl oz)

- ▶ 1 pub measure of spirits (25ml/1fl oz)

Latest Developments

In spite of the fact that all sorts of new information is emerging about diabetes you may find that your treatment still remains the same if the new dietary advice is not appropriate for you. In this section we look at the most up-to-date developments in dietary information about diabetes, so that you can be even better informed.

The Dose Adjustment For Normal Eating programme (DAFNE)

DAFNE is an educational programme for people with insulin-treated diabetes. It was developed in Germany in 1987 and it has been very successful in helping people with diabetes to manage their condition better. Several trials are currently under way in the UK to see if the benefits can be repeated here, but it is not available nationally.

On the programme, people with diabetes attend an intensive five-day course as part of a small group. They are encouraged to choose freely what they wish to eat and then taught to estimate the carbohydrate content for the quantity and type of foods and drinks chosen. They then adjust their insulin dose on a meal-by-meal basis as appropriate. In effect they are learning how to adapt their insulin to their lifestyle, not their lifestyle to their insulin.

Initial reports from both the UK and Germany have found that for adults with moderate to poor diabetes control, training in DAFNE seems to improve blood glucose levels compared with standard care. The studies have also found a reduction in frequency of hypo-glycaemia with effects lasting over several years of treatment.

Prior to the introduction of DAFNE, the dietary restrictions imposed on people with type 1 diabetes affected their overall quality of life. People using DAFNE now say that they enjoy more flexibility and the freedom to eat what and when they like. Furthermore, it has been noted that self-esteem improves. In DAFNE, participants learn from each other as well as from the facilitators and for many it is the first chance they have had to take time out to concentrate on managing their own diabetes.

Are there any problems associated with DAFNE?

Some people have some difficulty in dealing with the complexities of the carbohydrate-counting and in grasping the principles involved. In some cases, it is also necessary to increase the number of insulin injections. Two background doses of medium-/long-acting insulin are needed at the start and end of the day, along with another injection for each meal or snack. In addition, very intense blood glucose monitoring is encouraged which can be inconvenient at times.

The course does call for considerable commitment on the part not only of the participant but also of the facilitators. Time away from work, school or home may be required in order to participate.

Is DAFNE also used for type 2 diabetes?

DAFNE has also been tested for people with insulin-treated type 2 diabetes in Germany but the results have not yet been fully evaluated. The types of diabetes are very different in many ways and there are factors such as insulin resistance (see page 9) and the effects of physical activity which make treatment more complex.

Folic acid and the heart

Folic acid (sometimes referred to as folate) is a water-soluble B vitamin. Interest in it has grown in recent years since it was found to help prevent neural tube defects like spina bifida in babies. This is why women who are seeking to become pregnant and those in their first twelve weeks of pregnancy are advised to take a 400mcg supplement of folic acid each day.

However, did you know that it may also be helpful in reducing heart disease risk, which is a common complication of diabetes? Folic acid acts to lower the levels of a substance known as homocysteine in the blood. High levels of homocysteine are a risk factor for development of heart disease, stroke and peripheral vein disease.

Sources of folic acid

Folic acid occurs naturally in many foods including fruit (especially oranges and orange juice), vegetables (dark leafy veg such as broccoli, sprouts and spinach), potatoes, beans, pulses, wholegrains, milk and yogurt. It is also added to many refined cereal-based foods (indeed all cereal foods in the USA are now routinely fortified with it) and soft-grain bread (check the labels) – yet another good reason for people with diabetes to eat more of these foods.

Chromium and diabetes

Chromium is a trace mineral needed by the body in very small amounts. It helps in the maintenance of normal blood sugar levels, mainly by enhancing the action of insulin. It also seems to play a part in maintaining healthy cholesterol levels and in weight control.

People with a deficiency of chromium can develop impaired glucose tolerance (see page 9), which is improved by chromium supplementation. However, chromium is found naturally in a wide range of foods and most people with type 2 diabetes do not seem to be chromium-deficient, nor do they appear to be any more at risk of developing a deficiency. Nevertheless this has led researchers to question whether supplements may be of benefit to people with diabetes.

Studies have been carried out using large doses of chromium at a level far above that which could be obtained by diet alone. Few of the studies are well designed and controlled and the results are somewhat mixed. Some studies, notably in people with type 2 diabetes living in China, found that very high

doses of chromium led to an improved blood sugar control. However it is not clear if these findings would be applicable in other countries.

Many other studies have either been inconclusive or have shown no benefit. Research in the UK looked at moderate doses of chromium, such as could be obtained from diet, but found no benefit to glucose tolerance or blood fat levels in adults with type 2 diabetes.

Clearly more research is needed in order for the role of chromium to become clear. At present most diabetes organisations around the world do not recommend supplements. Current guidelines from Diabetes UK are that chromium should only be given as a supplement where a clear deficiency has been diagnosed. Otherwise people with type 2 diabetes should try to follow a healthy and varied diet including known sources of chromium (see the table below) in order to rule out the possibility of deficiency.

Sources of chromium

ANIMAL SOURCES	VEGETABLE SOURCES
Lean meat	Wholegrains
Offal, especially liver	Brewers' yeast
Oysters	Nuts and seeds
	Vegetables and pulses

Recipe Tips for Diabetes

All the recipes in this book are in line with healthy eating principles and they generally use low-fat, low-glycaemic index ingredients as appropriate. At times you will find that some dishes may appear to be 'no-go areas' for people with diabetes, but we want to dispel the myth that people with diabetes need a special diet. All your favourite foods can be incorporated into a healthy way of eating – it's getting the combinations right that's important and making sure that you choose a variety. Tempting desserts and main meals cooked in creamy sauces may sound off limits, but these recipes have been originated with diabetes in mind, using ingredients such as lean meat, fromage frais, half-fat crème fraîche, lower-fat Greek yogurt and skimmed milk. Asian-style dishes are served with steamed rice rather than fried rice, and in some recipes fat has been trimmed off meat after cooking, such as in Bacon Bollito (page 120), so that the fat content will actually be lower than in the analysis given in the recipe.

Cooking tips

- ▶ Select lean cuts of meat and trim off visible fat. Try to cook meat without adding fat by grilling, roasting and braising. Avoid using the juices from roast meat for gravy.
- ▶ Remove the skin from poultry and remember that the thigh and leg pieces are highest in fat.
- ▶ Grill chops, sausages and burgers and allow the fat to drain off.

- ▶ If you need to fry foods, try a cooking-oil spray on a non-stick pan.
- ▶ Use complex carbohydrate foods such as bread, cereals, pasta and potatoes. Just watch the amount of fat you put on them: choose lower-fat spreads and dairy products.
- ▶ Remember the Mediterranean 'musts' (see page 10) – garlic, fruit, vegetables, fish, nuts, beans, lentils.
- ▶ Select foods with a low glycaemic index, (GI; see page 12). Foods that are high in soluble fibre, such as rye, granary and soft-grain white bread, peas, sweetcorn, beans, lentils, citrus fruits and porridge oats, all have a low GI. Pulses such as beans, sweetcorn, peas and lentils are generally low in fat and calories and help to fill you up.
- ▶ Include lots of fish and try to include oily fish such as salmon, herring and mackerel once a week. Choose drained, canned tuna in brine rather than in oil – the former has half the fat!
- ▶ Nuts, although high in fat, can be part of a healthy lifestyle. Research shows that a handful of peanuts or almonds can help to lower your risks of heart disease. Nuts are best used as an ingredient in a main meal rather than as a snack, especially if you are overweight.

GIVE THESE A MISS...	... AND TRY THESE INSTEAD!
Butter on bread	Bread dipped in a little olive oil and balsamic vinegar
Cheddar cheese	French Brie or low-fat soft cheese
Rich desserts	Fruity puddings
French fries or mashed potato	Whole potatoes boiled in their skins
Fatty meat	Lean meat, poultry without the skin, fish
Flaky pastry	Filo pastry with skimmed milk between layers
Mayonnaise	Reduced-calorie mayonnaise or fat-free dressings
Full-fat dairy products, e.g. full-fat milk/cheese, butter	Reduced-fat foods, e.g. semi-skimmed milk, half-fat cheese, reduced- or low-fat spread
Cooking oil for frying	Spray oil for greasing and shallow-frying, a little olive or rapeseed oil for stir-frying, sautéeing, etc.
Crisps and salty snacks	Home-made popcorn, Melba toasts, pretzels, bread sticks
Rich cakes	Scones, fruit loaf, sponge cake

Eating Out

In today's hectic lifestyle, food on the go is becoming more and more common, and keeping an eye on the fats and figures can often become quite difficult as a result. What's more, fast food isn't necessarily healthy food, and often convenience overtakes health. So what are the best choices you can make to fit in with the chaos of modern-day life?

Going for an Indian

Opt for chicken, prawn or vegetable dishes rather than lamb or beef, which tend to be higher in fat – tandoori chicken, with plain boiled rice and some cucumber raita is a good choice. Tikka dishes or a small portion of grilled kebabs make good starters. Opt for dhal (lentil) dishes instead of veggie curries. They tend to be less oily. Pilau rice is fried rice, often with coloured grains – order boiled rice to keep the calories low. Basmati rice also has a low GI (see page 12), which is good news.

Ask if your poppadam can be microwaved or grilled, and your chapatis or naan served dry.

Some restaurants refer to Indian cheese, paneer, as cottage cheese, but watch out as it's actually full-fat cheese.

The chippie

Thick-cut chips absorb less fat than thin-cut ones, as the thin ones have a larger surface area, but do watch out for those massive portion sizes at the local chippie. If you're really hungry, you're better off sharing a small portion of chips and making them into a 'chip butty' (no butter, of course). This will help to fill you up and reduce the amount of oil you have.

Try also bringing your chips home and sitting them on kitchen paper – if you want to microwave them, do so for a few seconds on the kitchen paper and see the fat soak in. You could take the batter off the fish, or if you want to be neat, place the fish, skin side down, on a plate. Use your fork and eat the top layer of batter with the fish only, leaving the skin side on the plate.

For a healthier option, go for grilled fish if available, tomato sauce, bread roll and a salad accompaniment.

Burger binge

The fat content of the classic mega-size burgers is variable, as often they are fried. Top this with a dressing and cheese and the calories start to soar. It can still be acceptable on occasions, however, unless you pile on the fries and soft drink, in which case things do start to get a little out of hand. And the veggie-burger option is not necessarily any more virtuous. This is generally still cooked in fat and served with a creamy dressing.

Choose thick-cut chips where possible and ask for a regular-sized portion rather than a large one, which will save you half the calories.

Order diet drinks (around 10 teaspoons less sugar than regular) and ask for 'no dressing' and/or 'no cheese' and you could make a difference to the fat content. Ketchup is preferable to the creamy sauces.

Finally, munch through an apple or banana before going to the burger bar, otherwise you might be tempted to go for a large!

Going Greek

Order grilled fish, grilled lean lamb or a kebab. Traditional Greek staples, such as moussaka, taramasalata and hummus are high in fat and loaded with calories. Fill up on tzatziki – a low-fat mixture of yogurt, cucumber and garlic – with a small piece of pitta bread, instead. Undressed Greek salad without the feta cheese can also be very satisfying. Drizzle on some fresh lime juice and smother in coarsely ground black pepper.

A veggie option like falafel is usually deep-fried and therefore not necessarily lower in calories. Have fewer falafel balls and fill the pitta bread with some tzatziki and loads of salad.

Chinese food

A common pitfall when eating Chinese, Indian and Thai meals is ordering group dishes. Try to give yourself a full plate at the beginning of a meal and stop when it's finished. Pile up the salad and vegetables as they help to fill you up.

Order plain boiled rice or noodles rather than the special fried varieties. Soft noodles with vegetables (such as a chow mein dish) are preferable to crispy ones. Go for steamed dishes, like a whole steamed fish with ginger, steamed vegetables and steamed rice. Choose healthy starters like satay dishes with chilli dipping sauce, and finish with fresh fruit or a scoop of ice cream rather than the fried fritters.

Pasta and pizza

Remember that pasta has a low GI (see page 12), so order it often. Ask for a fresh tomato sauce, which tends to be lower in fat than cream-based sauces, and say 'no' to the Parmesan cheese. Even the smallest, thinnest restaurant pizzas have around 500 kilocalories, so go for a thin-base pizza with masses of vegetable toppings. Steer clear of extra cheese, pepperoni and deep-pan bases.

Veggie eating

It's often thought that vegetarian foods are healthier, but this is not always the case. Dishes that are based on eggs and cheese can be high in fat – Cheddar cheese, for example, has around 30 per cent fat, mostly saturated. And don't be fooled into thinking that all foods bought from a health-food shop are good for you. Many can be high in fat and sugar, and even though they may have been made with wholemeal flour, they are not necessarily healthy.

If you are vegetarian, pulse vegetables such as beans and lentils provide a valuable source of protein and have a low GI (see page 12). Use these together with starchy foods like rice and pasta to prepare perfectly balanced meals (see the table on page 18).

Shopping

As we have seen so far, diabetes is about sensible and varied eating habits – not specialist health-food shopping. Imagine your supermarket trolley is divided into thirds. One third should be made up of fruit and vegetables; another should consist of bread, other cereals and potatoes. The rest of the trolley should contain equal amounts of meat and fish, milk and dairy food and even less fatty or sugary food. So try to spend more time looking at the variety of fruit and vegetables and starchy cereals available and less time on fatty snack foods. This will help you to make healthy choices and will also add variety to your diet. Some people find that shopping on the Internet stops them from buying foods from less healthy aisles, as they are not tempted by the smells of the bakery.

What about convenience foods?

We are all tempted, at one time or another, by the myriad convenience foods on offer, be they ready meals, pasta sauces or desserts. Can they really be part of a healthy diet? Is it possible to mix and match to make them healthy?

Once again, it's all about balance and moderation. Many will be lower in starchy carbohydrate and fibre than home-made versions. If you find that this is the case, you can complement them with some extra grainy bread or a jacket potato. Another good tip is to get into the habit of serving them with extra vegetables or salad.

You may be concerned that quick or convenient foods may be high in fat, sugar and salt, all of which are relatively cheap ways for manufacturers to add flavour. But how can you tell? Sometimes it's easiest to look out for the 'healthy eating' logo used by all the major supermarkets, but you should take extra care with labels boasting 'healthy' on desserts and cakes, as they might be lower in fat but also higher in sugar, which does not necessarily mean that they are lower in calories.

Food labelling

Many foods make nutritional claims on their labels but research shows that consumers are very dubious as to how useful they really are. By law there are specific requirements a product must meet in order make a nutritional or nutrient claim, and these are shown in the table below. Such claims may indicate a healthier choice, but bear in mind that this is all relative, as a reduced-fat version of a high-fat food could still be a high source of fat.

In the past, manufacturers have sometimes added to the confusion by using 'per cent fat-free' claims, but an '85 per cent fat-free' food will still contain a hefty 15 per cent fat! Nowadays this misleading practice has been controlled, with the exception of the reasonable '97 per cent fat-free' claim on some products which contain only 3 per cent fat.

Guidelines to common nutrient claims (Food Standards Agency 2002)

NUTRITIONAL CLAIM	DEFINITION (PER 100G OR 100ML)	EXAMPLE
Low sugar Low fat Low sodium	Contains less than 5g sugar Contains less than 3g fat Contains less than 40mg sodium	Sugar-free custard Low-fat rice pudding Low-salt foods
Reduced sugar Reduced fat Reduced salt	Contains 25 per cent less sugar, fat or salt than standard product	Reduced-sugar jams Reduced-fat spreads Reduced-salt baked beans
Sugar free	Contains less than 0.2g sugar	Sugar-free jellies Sugar-free squashes Sugar-free fizzy drinks (may be called 'diet')
No added sugar/ unsweetened	Contains no sugars or no added foods that are composed mainly of sugars	Unsweetened fruit juices

Understanding nutritional information on food labels

Whilst the ingredients list will tell you what's in a food, it does not tell you how much. Ingredients are listed in descending order of weight, so the first ingredient will be present in the largest quantity and the last ingredient will be the smallest. This can be useful up to a point but the actual nutritional content is far more relevant. Even if sugar is near the top of the list, it does not necessarily mean that the food in question is packed with sugar. (Also remember that sugar does come in different guises, such as sucrose, dextrose, glucose syrup, maltose, etc.; see the table on page 12.)

The Guideline Daily Amounts (GDAs) listed on food labels provide information on the average recommended nutrient content in a healthy diet for an adult of normal body weight. Exact needs will vary between individuals according to age, weight and physical activity level. Nevertheless GDAs can help you to see how and whether a particular food might fit into your diet.

How do you compare foods?

Nutritional information can be used to tell you whether a food has a little or a lot of the listed nutrients. The table below provides guidelines to help you to determine this.

When looking at food labels it is good practice to consider how often and in what amounts you would normally eat the food. A food may be high in fat and/or sugar, but if you eat only small amounts of it occasionally, that's acceptable. For such foods you should refer to the 'per 100g' value; this is also useful for comparing two similar products such as ready-made sauces to see which is healthier. In the case of foods that you eat more frequently or in larger amounts, it is more appropriate to use the 'per serving' value.

Guideline Daily Amounts of nutrients for adults

NUTRIENT	MEN	WOMEN
Fat	95g	70g
Saturated fat	30g	20g
Sugar	70g	50g
Salt	7g	5g
Fibre	20g	16g

How to judge how much of a particular ingredient a food contains

A LOT	A LITTLE
20g fat	3g fat
5g saturates	1g saturates
10g sugars	2g sugars
0.5g sodium	0.1g sodium
1.5g salt	0.3g salt
3g fibre	0.5g fibre

Healthy shopping tips

▶ Watch out for ever-increasing portion sizes on ready meals and snacks such as sandwiches, crisps and chocolate bars. Just switching from a standard bag of crisps to a large bag would cause up to 6kg (13½lb) in weight gain over a year without changing anything else!

▶ Tinned foods such as fruit, vegetables, pulses and fish can be useful. Look for those labelled 'reduced' or 'no added' sugar or salt.

▶ Don't forget dried and frozen foods too – often just as nutritious and more convenient.

▶ Try to avoid shopping when you're hungry. Shop after a meal, make a shopping list and stick to it.

▶ Avoid foods such as biscuits and chocolates labelled 'suitable for diabetics'. They are usually expensive and have limited nutritional benefit. Since these are unlikely to form a major part of what you eat, you'd be better off just having a small amount of a standard product.

▶ Many supermarkets provide leaflets for people with diabetes, guiding them to healthy choices. Some even organise 'store tours' run by local registered dietitians. Consumers find these informative, enjoyable and a great way to view their regular store in a different light. Why not approach the customer services desk at your local store about this to generate demand?

Weight Management

Perhaps surprisingly, a heavy person burns more calories than a light person does, which destroys the myth that overweight people burn fewer calories when they exercise – often people who are overweight will blame their situation on a slow metabolism. It is possible to boost your metabolism by combining aerobic exercise and strength exercises.

Calories

The term 'calorie' is loosely used to describe the energy value of a food when the body burns it up. However, when talking about the measurement of energy, and hence how many calories a food has, the term kilocalories (or kcals) is more appropriate. On food labels, you will notice that the calorific value is given as kj/100g and kcal/100g. This means that every 100 grams of that product will provide you with the given amount of energy in kilojoules (kJ or kjoules) or kilocalories. One kcalorie is equivalent to 4.2 kjoules.

All the foods you eat provide calories, but some, generally those that are high in fat, are more concentrated in calories. For example, an apple, which is low in fat and high in fibre, will contain around 50 kcals, whereas an equivalent weight of Cheddar cheese will provide around eight times as many. Each gram of pure fat provides 9 kcals, whereas a gram of protein or a gram of carbohydrate will provide around 4 kcals. This is why frying a food can have a significant effect on the total calorie value.

Are you in shape?

Your ideal weight range depends on your height, and dietitians and doctors use each individual's body mass index (BMI) to calculate this. To find your BMI, take your weight (in kilograms) and divide it by your height (in metres squared):

$$BMI = \frac{weight\ (kg)}{height\ (m)^2}$$

The most desirable range is a BMI of between 20 and 24. A larger BMI is taken as an indication of being overweight and the higher that figure is, the more overweight you are.

The 'fruit salad' theory

Are you an 'apple', that is someone whose waist is bigger than their hips, or a 'pear', someone whose hips are bigger than their waist?

This may sound unimportant, but in fact real scientific theories have been formulated using this information. Central obesity, or putting weight on around the abdomen, is said to be associated with resistance to insulin, which in turn has been shown to be a risk factor in coronary heart disease (see Syndrome X, page 9). People with a higher waist measurement have a raised risk of diabetes and heart disease. A waist measurement of more than 94cm (37in) for men and more than 82cm (32in) in women is considered to carry a risk. Men of South Asian origin have been found to be even more at risk, so ideal waist measurements in their case need to be less than 92cm (36in).

It would therefore appear that being more pear-shaped may actually offer some protection. Eating well and taking regular physical activity can help to reduce excess abdominal fat.

Steps to success

Before you begin your new healthy lifestyle, make a list of all the positive benefits you feel it will give you. Your list may include things like helping you to fit into those old jeans, being able to run for the bus (and catch it!), looking and feeling more confident, feeling less breathless, getting your blood cholesterol down so you don't need tablets, and so on. Think about what this new lifestyle, physique, and so on, will do for you. How will a new image affect other areas of your life – your confidence, your work performance, your social life, your belief in yourself? And how will it affect the way in which you interact with others – family, friends and colleagues?

If you are absolutely clear about why you would like a healthier lifestyle, you will vastly increase your motivation and therefore your chances of success.

A practical approach

Follow the nutritional guidelines in this book to help you achieve a balanced intake of the right types of foods. Start by making a note of exactly what you're eating (a food diary), so that you have a written record of days when perhaps things could have gone better. If you couple this with notes about how you were feeling at that particular time, a connection may begin to emerge between your moods and the times when you indulge. This can be useful in helping you to make lasting changes.

There's no need to cook separately for yourself. The best part about eating the right foods for slimming is that they're also great foods for the whole family. Simply serve yourself smaller portions and fill up on the vegetables and starchy foods. Don't skip meals, as this often makes you ravenous by the next meal and you're more likely to overdo it, or to snack on high-calorie foods in between.

A healthy diet, tailored to your own individual needs may not sound as revolutionary as some of the 'miracle' diets endorsed by celebrities, but the evidence shows that it is the best way of losing weight sensibly and keeping it off. Registered dietitians can assess your current eating habits and lifestyle and advise you on appropriate strategies to lose weight slowly but steadily.

Think slim

▶ Often, keeping to a food plan means that you focus so much on food that you forget about the benefits of physical activity. Find ways of making exercise a part of your daily life in order to lose weight more quickly. Go for a brisk walk with a friend, splash around in the swimming pool or work out at the gym. Or, if you find it hard to make time for exercise, try running up and down the stairs at work a few times a day; or at home, jog on the spot whilst watching your favourite soap.

▶ If you find yourself battling with food cravings, you have two choices: either eat a small amount, enjoy it and move on, getting quickly back on track. Or, think about how much slimmer and fitter you will be if you keep going, and decide that you won't be defeated by a chunk of cake which would probably disappear in seconds and be nothing more than a 'quick fix'.

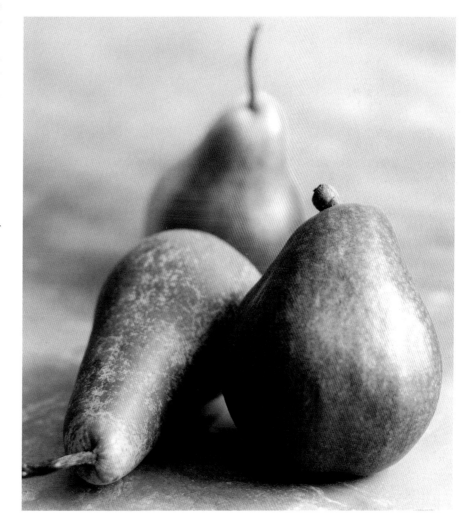

Keep a 'thoughts' diary. Write down what you eat, when you eat it and what you were thinking at the time. You might find that the foods you would ideally like to eat less of creep into the menu when you're feeling low, fed up or bored. An awareness that you fall into this trap at certain times can help you to stay on track by planning ahead. When you feel down, do other things besides eating to pick yourself up – go for a stroll, listen to some music, phone someone for a chat, soak in the bath, read a magazine – anything that you enjoy that will give you more positive thoughts.

Keep an eye on your eating habits. What time do you eat? Do you eat when you're hungry, or because, for example, it's mid-morning and everyone else is munching something. Are you a night-time snacker? If so, you could look at other ways of occupying yourself in the evenings to distract you from food. And if you must eat at night, choose healthier options, such as fruit, crudités with low-fat dips, fromage frais, diet yogurts, two crackers with a sliver of Cheddar cheese, a couple of Jaffa cakes or a handful of twiglets. Eat from a smaller plate to make your meals look bigger.

List all of the benefits that you hope to enjoy when you are fitter and healthier (see page 32). If you catch yourself straying, simply refer to your list and remind yourself of what you could achieve. Keep your list by the fridge, or anywhere eye-catching to keep you motivated.

Get physical

Physical activity helps your body to release endorphins, natural painkillers, which can in turn help you to combat stress and feel more energised. You don't need to jog ten times around the park or go to the gym every day in order to stay fit. Just try to incorporate simple activities into your daily lifestyle and gradually try to work up to 30 minutes a day, five times a week.

- Walk to the pillar box, take the dog out more often, take the kids for a brisk walk or simply park the car a bit farther away from your destination. Try to walk at a pace that leaves you slightly out of breath.
- Use the stairs instead of the lift whenever possible, or run up and down the steps at home a few times a day.
- Try skipping or jogging on the spot whilst watching TV.
- Take up a sport that you enjoy and which fits into your routine. Swimming with the kids or line dancing classes with a friend can be a fun way of working out.
- Remember that activity can be therapeutic, so tackling those garden weeds can have more benefits than you think.

And if you feel like giving it all up, take a look at your list of how great you'll feel when you get there and simply start again. You're human – it's perfectly acceptable to have 'off' days.

Keeping healthy – for life

In June 2002 the Diabetes Research and Wellness Foundation launched 'Think Well to be Well', a new concept in caring for people with diabetes. Bringing a fresh approach to diet and diabetes, the concept helps people with diabetes to take control of their life and to focus on achieving sustainable results. Let's take a look now at some practical steps based on this concept, which will allow you to challenge your thinking, helping you to achieve more long-term results.

Old habits die hard...

...so they say. But it's actually making that decision to make the change that takes longer. So start today by changing your attitude and you'll soon find other things changing with it.

What should you say to yourself?

The way you think can have a dramatic effect on your behaviour, including what you eat. The instructions that you feed your mind are what the mind will respond to. Practise giving yourself positive reinforcement and encourage-ment. Link these thoughts directly with your goal. For example, say things like, 'I feel better about myself when I eat fruit after lunch', or 'I'm doing well by walking more'. Imagine what others might say to support you, that would give you a positive feeling.

Your mind is programmed to give you more of whatever you are thinking about, so if you're thinking about being fat or unfit you are inadvertently programming yourself to get what you don't want. Tennis players, for example, know that if they worry about hitting the ball into the net, that is exactly where it is likely to go, so they focus on getting the ball just where they want it to go. The trick is to make conscious choices that bring you closer to your goal, in this case achieving a healthy lifestyle.

Keeping your diabetes in check
- ▶ Quit smoking now.
- ▶ Keep to recommended foods most of the time. The more low-GI (see page 12), balanced foods you eat, the better. Choose foods you enjoy and which fit in with your lifestyle, so that any changes are sustainable.
- ▶ Make sure you incorporate regular physical activity into your daily habits. This could be as simple as walking up the stairs, or parking the car a little farther away from your destination than normal.
- ▶ Keep to your prescribed dose of medication, unless it has been recommended by your medical advisers that you make changes.
- ▶ Check your blood glucose regularly so you can assess how your diabetes is at any given time.

- ▶ Attend your clinic for regular check-ups, and make sure that you monitor the health of your feet and eyes.
- ▶ Take appropriate action during periods of illness, or when going on holiday.
- ▶ Keep to within the maximum daily limits of alcohol (see page 23).
- ▶ Find ways of relaxing that will help you to combat stress.

Keeping the weight off
So you've done well and reached your desired weight. The last thing you want to do now is to put all that weight back on. But the sad fact is that most people who lose weight do regain it. So how can you make sure that doesn't happen to you? If your weight-reducing diet is something that you simply put up with until you reach your goal, then maybe it's the wrong diet for you. Seeing it as an endurance test is likely to make you indulge when it's over, which tends to make you fall back into those old habits. And then, of course, the weight creeps back on again.

Here are some 'think slim' tips:
- ▶ Treat your slimming plan as a new way of life. You may lapse occasionally – that's fine. Just acknowledge it and start again.
- ▶ Try to keep a sense of perspective about your weight – if you put on a pound or two, you can always take it off again.

- ▶ Challenge yourself. Now you have reached your target, what are you going to do next? Why not learn a new sport, or take up a new hobby?
- ▶ Find ways to make your work routine and your family support you. You are going to stay slim and healthy.
- ▶ Turn out your wardrobe and enjoy giving away clothes that are too big for you. Indulge yourself and buy some new clothes. If you make an effort to look good, you'll want to stay slim.
- ▶ Encourage your family and friends to join in with your exercise regime. It's much more fun to go cycling or swimming or play sport with other people.
- ▶ Keep a daily 'food and mood' diary so you can see when you indulge and what your emotions are up to at that time, e.g. boredom, stress, comfort, security, PMT.
- ▶ Before you reach for solace in that 'unhealthy nibble', ask yourself if choosing this is taking you nearer to the 'new' you, and if it isn't, choose again!
- ▶ Distract yourself. Perhaps make a creative list of all the things that would work for you, from going for a walk to having a bath or dancing to your favourite CD. By the time you've done this, your brain would have been sufficiently tricked into believing that it no longer needs that 'fix'!

For the past seven years, I've felt on top of the world. Memories of bronchitis, flu, colds and coughs had been dispatched by my new love of eating well and eating organic. Visits to the doctor were few and far between and I was starting to feel as if I was untouchable by disease or ailment.

All until I agreed to appear in a TV programme about sugar that involved having a test for Syndrome X (see page 9). I must have been mad – the things you do for telly! – but I knew a test this thorough was not available on the National Health Service. It was a complicated drawn-out test where glucose and insulin was pumped into my left arm and my right arm was placed in an 'oven' at 65°C (149°F). Blood was taken from it every 10 minutes for two hours and was then spun centrifugally to test my insulin resistance.

Shock, horror – I had Syndrome X; I was on my way to type 2 diabetes unless, that is, I took steps to change my lifestyle. With Syndrome X there is a way back, however, unlike with type 2.

It is estimated that between 20 and 25 per cent of the UK population has Syndrome X and they won't know a thing about it until it moves on to type 2 diabetes, and that will happen unless you take the right steps. Have a close look at your diet, take aerobic exercise to increase your heart rate for at least 20 minutes, four times a week, lose some of those pounds of flesh that seem to have come from nowhere and if you smoke, stop.

I have changed my lifestyle and hopefully I won't move on to the diabetes stage, but if I do then I'm determined still to enjoy my food. Wholesale changes aren't necessary; you can still eat normally – it's just that certain foods need restricting – or if instructed by your doctor, cutting out altogether. But this doesn't mean your diet has to be boring. With a little imagination and a good knowledge of the dos, don'ts, whys and wherefores, life shouldn't really have to change that much.

Although I have written this book for people with diabetes, there is no harm in everyone getting stuck in too. Many of us need to watch what we eat, so there is no reason why you shouldn't have a lifestyle change straight away; an AWT meal a day may well keep Syndrome X away.

I'll be honest: out of choice I wouldn't use artificial sweeteners that contain aspartame, but natural substitutes for sugar are slowly finding their way on to the market. Even with Syndrome X I prefer not to use margarines or spreads containing trans fats or hydrogenated vegetable oils as there is more and more evidence that these can harm your health, but there are recipes in this book where there is no substitute. And I won't encourage you to drink artificially sweetened colas for the same reason, as you should try to discover more natural drinks. You can help yourself without reverting to science; natural foods unenhanced with chemicals are always going to be a better choice.

None of my recipes requires rocket science. Here are simple 'normal' recipes using a little knowledge and a lot of imagination to keep you enjoying your food. There is no regime, just common sense; no sergeant major barking orders, just foodie pleasure. Azmina has already explained the best balance of foods to eat. Remember that each meal should contain vegetables and starchy carbohydrates. Follow Azmina's advice and you'll soon realise that being diagnosed with diabetes need not be a trial or a long-term foodie prison sentence. Life is for living so give yourself that chance.

Breakfasts and Brunches

1

Asparagus, smoked bacon and spring onion hash
Perfect for a late brunch or lazy lunch, this classic dish combines great flavours with great textures.
Serves 2

1 garlic clove, finely chopped
2 spring onions, sliced into 2.5cm (1in) pieces
50g (2oz) lean smoked bacon, diced
½ tablespoon rapeseed oil
1 teaspoon capers, drained and rinsed

8 cooked asparagus spears, cut into 5cm (2in) pieces
1 tablespoon black olives, pitted and diced
1 tablespoon balsamic vinegar
3 eggs
Freshly ground black pepper

In a non-stick pan, fry the garlic, spring onions and bacon in the oil until golden. Add the capers, asparagus, olives and vinegar and heat through.

Whisk the eggs and pour into the asparagus mix. Stir until the eggs are cooked to your liking and take on a scrambled appearance.

Season with black pepper to taste and serve on granary toast.

Per serving: 203 kcals, 14g fat, 4g saturated fat, 3g carbohydrate, 0.83g sodium

Salmon and kipper kedgeree
A pleasant alternative to the usual smoked haddock version. Traditionally a recipe served at breakfast, this also makes a great light lunch, but eat once a week or so, rather than everyday. **Serves 2**

1 kipper fillet
175g (6oz) salmon fillet
1 bay leaf
150g (5oz) brown rice
½ onion, chopped
25g (1oz) unsalted butter

2 teaspoons curry paste
2 eggs, hard-boiled and chopped
2 tablespoons chopped parsley
Freshly ground black pepper

Cook the kipper and salmon in 600ml (1 pint) water with the bay leaf over a medium heat for 7 minutes, then allow to cool slightly. Discard the bay leaf and lift the fish out of the water, reserving the water. Flake the fish, discarding any skin or bone.

Rinse the rice, then measure 1 cup rice to 3 cups reserved fish cooking water into a pan, bring to the boil, reduce the heat and simmer covered, for about 30 minutes. Drain, separate the grains with a fork and set aside.

Meanwhile, cook the onion slowly in the butter until soft but not browned, add the curry paste and stir to combine. Add the rice, flaked fish, hard-boiled eggs and parsley and stir. Season with black pepper to taste and serve immediately.

Per serving: 766 kcals, 40g fat, 12g saturated fat, 64g carbohydrate, 0.73g sodium

Scrambled eggs and smoked salmon timbales
A classic dish, but given a more chef-style presentation. Two ingredients that combine to make the perfect breakfast. **Serves 2**

Rapeseed-oil spray (see page 17)

110g (4oz) smoked salmon, thinly sliced

4 eggs

2 teaspoons horseradish sauce

2 teaspoons snipped chives

Freshly ground black pepper

10g (½oz) unsalted butter

Watercress, to garnish

Lemon wedges, to garnish

Lightly spray 4 timbales with oil and line with clingfilm.
Line each timbale with strips of smoked salmon, making sure there are no gaps and leaving an overhang to create a lid once the timbales are filled with scrambled eggs.
Lightly beat the eggs, folding in the horseradish and chives, but keeping some viscosity (in other words, don't overbeat). Season with pepper.
Melt the butter in a non-stick frying pan or saucepan until it foams, then pour in the eggs. With a wooden spoon, draw the edges of the eggs into the centre continuously until they have cooked to your liking. Immediately spoon the scrambled eggs into the smoked salmon moulds, push the eggs down with a teaspoon, then fold over the smoked salmon to enclose.
Turn the moulds out into the centre of 2 plates and garnish with any excess smoked salmon, the watercress and lemon wedges.

Per serving: 277 kcals, 18g fat, 6g saturated fat, 2g carbohydrate, 1.22g sodium

Baked egg in herbed roast beefsteak tomato
Eggs with inspiration. A wonderfully rich and filling dish, and the dash of Martini gives it a touch of decadence. **Serves 4**

50g (2oz) button mushrooms, finely chopped

1 small onion, finely chopped

½ teaspoon soft thyme leaves

½ teaspoon ground black pepper

1 tablespoon olive oil

1 tablespoon dry Martini

4 beefsteak tomatoes

5 eggs

2 tablespoons low-fat Greek yogurt

2 teaspoons snipped chives

2 teaspoons finely chopped flat parsley

Freshly ground black pepper

In a saucepan, cook the mushrooms, onion, thyme and black pepper in the olive oil on a gentle heat for about 15 minutes, stirring regularly until the onions have softened and the vegetables have released most of their liquid. Add the Martini and boil until all the liquid has evaporated, then set aside to keep warm.
Preheat the oven to 180°C/350°F/gas mark 4.
Cut 1cm (½in) from the rounded end of each tomato. Hollow out the seeds and discard. Place the tomatoes cut side up on a roasting tray and cook for 10 minutes in the oven, with the lids placed separately on the roasting tray.
Meanwhile, beat one of the eggs. Whisk together the yogurt, herbs, 1 tablespoon water and the beaten egg. Remove the tomatoes from the oven and place a quarter of the mushroom mix in the bottom of each hollowed-out tomato. Break a raw egg on to the mushroom mix, spoon the yogurt mix over the egg and top each tomato with a tomato lid.
Return to the oven and cook for 10–15 minutes depending on how well you like your eggs cooked.

Per serving: 161 kcals, 11g fat, 3g saturated fat, 6g carbohydrate, 0.11g sodium

Scrambled crab

Eggs and crab make an excellent partnership and a more unusual combination than scrambled eggs and salmon. White meat comes from the claw of the crab and is the tastiest. **Serves 2**

4 eggs
100g (3½oz) white crab meat
Freshly ground black pepper
2 slices wholegrain bread
10g (½oz) unsalted butter
2 tablespoons low-fat Greek yogurt

Lightly beat the eggs, then combine with the crab meat. Season with ground black pepper. Toast the bread and spread with half of the butter. Keep warm.

Heat the remaining butter in a non-stick frying pan, pour in the eggs and stir until cooked to how you like your eggs. Fold in the yogurt and spoon on to the buttered toast.

Per serving: 337 kcals, 19g fat, 7g is saturated fat, 15g carbohydrate, 0.55g sodium

Brown soda bread

This is the easiest bread in the world to make. An Irish speciality, it is raised with bicarbonate of soda and an acid, the soured milk or buttermilk, instead of yeast. **Makes 1 loaf**

450ml (16fl oz) semi-skimmed milk or buttermilk
Juice of 1 lemon (if using milk)
280g (10oz) plain white flour
1 rounded teaspoon salt (optional)
1 rounded teaspoon bicarbonate of soda
280g (10oz) stone-ground wholemeal flour

Preheat the oven to 230°C/450°F/gas mark 8.

To sour the milk, pour it into a large jug with the lemon juice. Allow to stand for 15 minutes to thicken before stirring. If you prefer, you can use buttermilk instead of souring the milk yourself.

Sift the white flour, salt (if using) and bicarbonate of soda, then add the wholemeal flour, stirring to combine in a large bowl. Make a well in the centre and add the soured milk or buttermilk, little by little.

Working from the centre, combine the mixture either by hand or with a wooden spoon, adding more soured milk if necessary. The dough should be soft, but not sticky. If it becomes too wet, add more flour.

Turn out on to a floured board and knead lightly, just enough to shape into a round. Flatten slightly to about 5cm (2in) thick and place on a baking tray.

Using a floured large knife, mark a deep cross on top and bake in the oven for 15–20 minutes, then reduce the heat to 200°C/400°F/gas mark 6 for 20–25 minutes, or until the bread is cooked and the bottom sounds hollow when tapped.

Per quarter loaf: 508 kcals, 4g fat, 2g saturated fat, 105g carbohydrate, 0.75g sodium

Dried cherry muffins
Other dried fruit can be substituted, but I think that cherries are the most delicious. These muffins are great for a quick breakfast or mid-morning snack.

Makes 12 small muffins

150ml (5fl oz) semi-skimmed milk or buttermilk
1 tablespoon lemon juice (if using milk)
Rapeseed-oil spray (see page 17)
75g (3oz) dried pitted cherries

150g (5oz) plain flour
1½ teaspoons baking powder
50g (2oz) unsalted butter
75g (3oz) caster sugar
1 egg
½ teaspoon grated orange zest

Preheat the oven to 180°C/350°F/gas mark 4.

If using milk, combine it with the lemon juice and leave to stand for 30 minutes. Lightly spray a 12-cup muffin tin or 12 muffin paper cups with oil.

If you have time, soak the cherries in the milk mix or buttermilk for 30 minutes. I know it's breaking the rules and isn't essential, but it does help to soften the cherries.

In a large bowl, sift together the flour and baking powder.

In a separate bowl, cream together the butter and sugar until light and fluffy. Lightly beat the egg, then add to the creamed butter together with the orange zest and combine.

Make a well in the centre of the flour and baking powder and spoon in the cherries and soured milk or buttermilk. Add the butter mixture and mix the whole together with your hands until just combined. Don't overwork the batter.

Heap the mixture into the muffin cups, filling them two-thirds full. Bake in the oven for about 20 minutes, or until a skewer or cocktail stick inserted into the centre comes out clean.

Transfer the muffins to a wire rack to cool.

Per muffin: 131 kcals, 5g fat, 3g saturated fat, 22g carbohydrate, 0.09g sodium

Honey, orange and thyme bran muffins
There is plenty of fibre, but very little fat in these delicious muffins. Wheatbran is available from good health-food shops. **Makes 12 muffins**

150ml (5fl oz) semi-skimmed milk or buttermilk
1 tablespoon lemon juice (if using milk)
Rapeseed-oil spray (see page 17)
25g (1oz) soft light brown sugar
25g (1oz) unsalted butter, melted

2 eggs, lightly beaten
½ teaspoon soft thyme leaves
60ml (2fl oz) liquid honey
Grated zest of 2 oranges
225g (8oz) plain flour
225g (8oz) unprocessed wheat bran
1 tablespoon baking powder
Pinch of salt

If using the milk, combine it with the lemon juice and leave to stand for 30 minutes.

Lightly spray a 12-cup muffin tin or 12 muffin paper cups with oil.

Place the sugar in a bowl and combine with the melted butter, soured milk or buttermilk, eggs, thyme, honey and orange zest.

In another bowl, combine the flour, bran, baking powder and salt. Make a well in the dry ingredients and then fold in the milk mix. Combine until just mixed, but don't overwork the batter.

Fill each muffin cup two-thirds full with the batter and bake for 20–25 minutes until golden and cooked through. To test, insert a skewer into the centre of a muffin: if it comes out clean, the muffin is cooked. Remove from the oven, allow to stand for 10 minutes then turn the muffins out on to a wire rack to cool completely.

Per muffin: 161 kcals, 4g fat, 2g saturated fat, 27g carbohydrate, 0.24g sodium

2

Soups and Salads

Jerusalem artichoke soup

Jerusalem artichokes have nothing to do with Jerusalem or globe artichokes, but are a good part of a healthy diet. They also taste great raw and grated over salads. **Serves 4**

Olive-oil spray (see page 17)
450g (1lb) Jerusalem artichokes, peeled, diced and submerged in acidulated water (water with a little lemon juice or vinegar added)
1 onion, diced
225g (8oz) floury potatoes, diced
2 garlic cloves, finely chopped
1 celery stick, diced

1 heaped teaspoon soft thyme leaves
1 litre (1¾ pints) chicken or vegetable stock
150ml (5fl oz) skimmed milk
4 tablespoons low-fat Greek yogurt
Pinch of freshly grated nutmeg
50g (2oz) tender young spinach leaves
Freshly ground black pepper

Lightly spray a pan with olive oil. Drain the artichokes and add them to the pan. Add the onion, potatoes, garlic, celery and thyme, then stir to combine. Cover with a lid and cook for 10 minutes, shaking the pan occasionally, until the potatoes have started to soften but not colour.

Pour the stock into the pan, bring to the boil, then reduce to a simmer and cook for another 10 minutes or so until all the vegetables have softened and are completely tender. Leave to cool a little and then blend in batches using a hand-held mixer or food processor until smooth. If you would like a squeaky-smooth soup, pass through a fine sieve. Return the soup to the pan.

Add the milk and yogurt to the pan, whisk to combine, then add the nutmeg and spinach and reheat gently, stirring, until the spinach has wilted. Season with black pepper to taste and ladle into warmed soup bowls. Serve at once with crusty wholegrain bread.

Per serving: 164 kcals, 2g fat, 1g saturated fat, 32g carbohydrate, 0.39g sodium

Watercress and potato soup

A classic French combination that tastes wonderful and also does you good. This is warm and thick soup, perfect for the winter months.

Serves 4

2 shallots, finely diced
1 sprig thyme
25g (1oz) unsalted butter
2 bunches watercress, leaves and stalks separated
325g (11½oz) floury potatoes, diced

1.2 litres (2 pints) vegetable or chicken stock, boiling
4 tablespoons low-fat yogurt
Freshly ground black pepper

In a pan, cook the shallots and thyme gently in the butter until softened but not coloured. Tie the watercress stalks together with string, then put in the pan. Add potatoes and stir to combine.

Add the boiling stock and cook aggressively until the potatoes are soft. Remove the watercress stalks and discard.

Add half the watercress leaves, cook for a further minute, then liquidise in a blender. Pass the puréed soup through a fine sieve. Whisk in the yogurt and the remaining watercress leaves. Heat through and season with black pepper before serving.

Per serving: 123 kcals, 6g fat, 3g saturated fat, 13g carbohydrate, 0.43g sodium

Cold pea and mint soup with a broad bean salad *A perfect light summer lunch.*

Use fresh podded peas when in season, but to be honest, frozen peas are just as nutritious. **Serves 4**

900ml (1¾ pints) vegetable
    stock
1 garlic clove, crushed
4 spring onions, sliced
1 tablespoon vegetable oil
450g (1lb) podded peas (fresh
    or frozen)
1 tablespoon caster sugar
2 tablespoons chopped mint
    leaves
Freshly ground black pepper
150ml (5fl oz) low-fat Greek
    yogurt

For the broad bean salad
175g (6oz) broad beans,
    weighed after podding and
    skinning, or 400g (14oz)
    tinned white beans, drained
4 spring onions, finely sliced
1 tablespoon olive oil
1 teaspoon lemon juice
1 tablespoon grated Parmesan
    cheese

In a saucepan, bring the vegetable stock to the boil.

In separate saucepan, cook the garlic and spring onions in the vegetable oil until the onion is soft but not brown. Add the peas and sugar, then add the boiling stock. Cook for 12 minutes if you are using fresh peas, 4 minutes if frozen. Allow to cool.

In a liquidiser, blend the soup with the mint. Season with black pepper to taste, cool and refrigerate. When chilled, whisk in the yogurt.

To make the salad, just before serving combine the broad beans or white beans and spring onions with the olive oil and lemon juice. Season with plenty of ground pepper. Fold in the Parmesan.

Make a small pile of the salad in the centre of 4 soup plates, pour the soup around and serve immediately.

Per serving: 238 kcals, 11g fat, 3g saturated fat, 22g carbohydrate, 0.35g sodium

A warming rustic garlic soup *A soup to lift the heart, garlic is full of beneficial properties. It is antibacterial, and antiviral and may help to reduce blood cholesterol and nasal congestion.* **Serves 2**

5 garlic cloves, thinly sliced
25g (1oz) lean streaky bacon,
    finely diced (optional)
1 red chilli, finely sliced
1 onion, finely sliced
1 teaspoon soft thyme leaves

1 tablespoon olive oil
4 thick slices wholegrain bread,
    crusts removed
½ teaspoon paprika
600ml (1 pint) chicken stock
Freshly ground black pepper

In a saucepan cook the garlic, bacon, if using, chilli, onion and thyme in the olive oil until golden. Break the bread into small cubes and add to the pan with the paprika and chicken stock. **Bring** to the boil and simmer for 10 minutes, stirring from time to time until the bread has broken down and thickened the liquid. For a smoother soup, blend in a liquidiser or food processor. Season with black pepper to taste.

Per serving: 271 kcals, 8g fat, 1g saturated fat, 42g carbohydrate, 0.83g sodium

Toasted pasta in wild mushroom broth

This is the perfect soup to make in autumn or winter when wild mushrooms are at their best. A good source of carbohydrates. **Serves 4**

110g (4oz) wholewheat fettuccine

1 tablespoon olive oil

Olive-oil spray (see page 17)

1 teaspoon soft thyme leaves

1 teaspoon chopped garlic

2 onions, roughly chopped

25g (1oz) dried ceps or porcini, soaked in 300ml (10fl oz) boiling water

1 bunch parsley, leaves and stalks

1 teaspoon black peppercorns

1.2 litres (2 pints) vegetable or chicken stock

225g (8oz) mixed fresh wild mushrooms, cleaned

50g (2oz) button mushrooms, cleaned

Freshly ground pepper

1 bunch spring onions, sliced

Preheat the oven to 180°/350°F/gas mark 4.

Break the pasta into smaller pieces, toss in the oil and place on a baking sheet. Bake in the oven for 10 minutes until golden. Set aside to cool.

Spray a saucepan with a little olive oil and cook the thyme, garlic and onions over a medium heat for about 10 minutes or until the onion has softened, but not coloured. Add the soaked dried mushrooms with their liquid, the parsley stalks, the peppercorns and the stock, bring to the boil and cook for 30 minutes.

Meanwhile remove any stalks from the wild mushrooms and add them to the stock. Slice the mushroom caps, quarter the button mushrooms and set aside.

Strain the stock, wipe out the saucepan and return the strained liquid to the saucepan. Add the pasta and the prepared fresh mushrooms and cook for a further 10 minutes.

Season with black pepper to taste and sprinkle with spring onions. Serve very hot.

Per serving: 184 kcals, 5g fat, 1g saturated fat, 30g carbohydrate, 0.47g sodium

Tomato water

The ultimate slimming soup, this is also highly refreshing and light and well worth the effort. Presentation is everything here: the basil should float elegantly around the small tomato dice. **Serves 4**

1kg (2¼lb) ripe but firm vine tomatoes, roughly chopped

1 tablespoon Worcestershire sauce

1 teaspoon Tabasco sauce

½ cucumber, cut into chunks

300ml (10fl oz) Evian water

1 teaspoon salt

3 plum tomatoes, seeded and diced

6 basil leaves

Blend all the ingredients, except for the plum tomatoes and basil, in a liquidiser.

Pour the pulp into jelly bags and allow to drip through, preferably overnight. Do not force through as it will cloud the liquid. Chill until ready to serve.

Garnish each bowl with diced tomato and some chiffonade of shredded basil. Pour the tomato water over and serve immediately.

Per serving: 64 kcals, 1g fat, 0.1g saturated fat, 12g carbohydrate, 0.59g sodium

Grilled shellfish gazpacho
An exciting variation on a Spanish theme; gazpacho is usually a vegetarian soup, but here I have added prawns, scallops and crab meat.

Serves 4

1 slice wholegrain country
  bread, crusts removed and
  broken into small chunks
1 dessertspoon sherry vinegar
½ garlic clove, finely chopped
1 teaspoon caster sugar
½ red chilli, seeded, finely diced
2 tablespoons olive oil, plus
  extra for brushing
350g (12oz) plum tomatoes,
  peeled and seeded
200ml (7fl oz) tomato juice
2 spring onions, finely sliced

½ red pepper, roasted or grilled,
  peeled, seeded and diced
½ large cucumber, peeled,
  seeded and roughly diced
1 dessertspoon pesto
Freshly ground black pepper
3 large raw prawns, shelled
4 diver-caught scallops,
  shucked
Basil leaves to garnish
125g (4½oz) white crab meat

For the basil salt (optional)
Handful of basil leaves
125g (4½oz) Maldon salt

Place the bread in a food processor or blender. While blitzing the bread, add the vinegar, garlic, sugar and chilli and blend until smooth.

Add the olive oil, a little at a time, until it has been absorbed by the bread. Add the tomatoes, tomato juice, spring onions, red pepper, cucumber and pesto. Continue to blitz until a smooth emulsion is formed. Season to taste with black pepper.

To make the basil salt, place the ingredients in a food processor and blend until smooth and green. Store in an airtight container.

Half an hour before serving, sprinkle the prawns and scallops with ½ teaspoon of the basil salt, if desired, and toss to combine.

Dust off the salt from the prawns and scallops and brush with a little olive oil. Cook them under a hot grill or in a griddle or heavy-based frying pan for 1–2 minutes on each side.

Ideally serve in large-rimmed shallow soup bowls. Place the prawns and scallops in the centre, then pour the soup around the shellfish. Scatter each bowl with basil leaves and fresh crab and serve immediately.

Per serving: 198 kcals, 10g fat, 2g saturated fat, 11g carbohydrate, 0.65g sodium

Poached shellfish in oriental broth
Another seafood speciality, this soup contains light, vibrant flavours, but with a little bite. A recipe with lots of Asian tastes.

Serves 4

1 tablespoon vegetable oil
1 teaspoon Thai red curry
  paste
2 garlic cloves, sliced
1 onion, thinly sliced
½ fennel head, thinly sliced
1 tablespoon tomato purée
1 lemongrass stalk, finely
  chopped
2 dried bird's eye chillies
1 kaffir lime leaf, shredded
  (optional)
1cm (½ in) piece of fresh root
  ginger, finely chopped
1 'petal' broken off a star anise
2 litres (3½ pints) fish stock
1 teaspoon chopped tarragon

For finishing the broth
110g (4oz) asparagus tips
50g (2oz) podded peas (fresh
  or frozen)
4 large diver-caught scallops
110g (4oz) salmon fillet, cut
  into 4 pieces
8 large shelled prawns, peeled
  and deveined
24 mussels, cleaned
110g (4oz) white crab meat
75g (3oz) sugar-snap peas
2 tomatoes, quartered and
  seeded
Juice of 2 limes
1 tablespoon nam pla (Thai
  fish sauce)
24 coriander leaves
Handful of baby spinach leaves

Heat the oil in a saucepan, add the curry paste and cook for 1 minute, stirring regularly. Add the garlic, onion and fennel and cook gently for 10 minutes.

Stir in the tomato purée, lemongrass, chillies, lime leaf (if using), ginger and star anise. Pour on the stock and add the tarragon. Simmer over a low heat for an hour, then strain the broth into a clean saucepan.

Bring the broth to the boil, add the asparagus and peas and cook for 2 minutes. Add the scallops and salmon and cook for a further 2 minutes. Add the remaining ingredients and cook until the mussels have opened. Ladle into 4 warm bowls.

Per serving: 241 kcals, 9g fat, 1g saturated fat, 10g carbohydrate, 1.26g sodium

A thai soup of whiting and squid

Whiting is an underused fish that is suited to Thai flavours. If you can't find it, you can use cod, haddock or monkfish instead.

Serves 6

1.5 litres (2½ pints) fish stock
1 lime, thinly sliced
2 kaffir lime leaves, finely
    shredded
3 garlic cloves, crushed
3 red chillies, thinly sliced
2½cm (1in) piece of fresh root
    ginger, sliced
1 lemongrass stalk, finely
    chopped
2 tablespoons nam pla (Thai
    fish sauce)

450g (1lb) whiting fillets, cut
    into 5cm (2in) cubes
225g (8oz) baby asparagus tips
4 spring onions, sliced
450g (1lb) squid tubes, cut
    into 5cm (2in) cubes
175g (6oz) sugar-snap peas
Freshly ground black pepper
2 tablespoons chopped
    coriander leaves

In a large saucepan, bring the stock to the boil and add the lime, lime leaves, garlic, chillies, ginger, lemongrass and nam pla. Simmer for 5 minutes.

Add the whiting, asparagus and spring onions and cook for a further 4 minutes. Then add the squid and peas and cook for just 1 more minute. Season with black pepper, garnish with the coriander leaves and serve immediately.

Per serving: 159 kcals, 2g fat, 0.1g saturated fat, 5g carbohydrate, 0.83g sodium

Chicken noodle soup

This version of a classic Chinese soup uses buckwheat noodles instead of egg noodles. As the soup contains plenty of carbs, it is best eaten as a main meal.

Serves 4

225g (8oz) buckwheat noodles
1 teaspoon sesame oil
1 teaspoon vegetable oil
½ teaspoon grated fresh root
    ginger
1 garlic clove, finely chopped
½ teaspoon chilli, diced
3 spring onions, sliced
4 tablespoons reduced-salt
    soy sauce

2 teaspoon liquid honey
1.2 litres (2 pints) chicken
    stock
Freshly ground black pepper
175g (6oz) cooked chicken,
    shredded
1 tablespoon chopped
    coriander leaves

Cook the noodles in boiling water until tender: this should take about 4 minutes. When the noodles are cooked, drain and refresh in cold water.

Meanwhile, in a saucepan, heat both the oils over a medium heat. Add the ginger, garlic, chilli and spring onions and cook for 3 minutes, stirring constantly. Add the soy sauce, liquid honey and chicken stock, then bring to the boil and simmer for 3 minutes. Season with black pepper to taste.

Add the noodles to the soup, then add the cooked chicken and coriander. Reheat for 2 minutes before serving.

Per serving: 326 kcals, 7g fat, 1g saturated fat, 47g carbohydrate, 1.06g sodium

Jewelled couscous
Usually an accompaniment to a Moroccan tagine, but it makes a delicious salad too. A version can also be made with rice. Either way, it is a light and colourful dish, rich in flavours. **Serves 2**

200ml (7fl oz) chicken or vegetable stock
1 tablespoon olive oil
½ teaspoon salt
110g (4oz) couscous
Finely grated zest of 1 unwaxed lemon
Juice of ½ lemon
25g (1oz) flaked almonds, toasted
50g (2oz) dried apricots, soaked in a little water for 20 minutes, drained and chopped
25g (1oz) sultanas or raisins
4 tablespoons roughly chopped flat parsley
4 tablespoons roughly chopped coriander

Heat the stock in a large pan with the olive oil and the salt. Bring to the boil and immediately remove from the heat. Pour in the couscous in a thin, steady stream and then stir in the lemon zest. Set aside for 10 minutes to allow the grains to swell and until the couscous has soaked up all of the liquid.

Return the couscous to the heat and drizzle over the lemon juice. Heat gently for about 5 minutes, stirring with a long-pronged fork to fluff up the grains, then remove from the heat.

Fold in the almonds, apricots, sultanas or raisins, parsley and coriander. Season with black pepper to taste. Serve with Chicken Tagine (see page 115) or allow to cool to room temperature and serve as a healthy salad.

Per serving: 343 kcals, 14g fat, 1g saturated fat, 49g carbohydrate, 0.64g sodium

North african pumpkin salad with garlic, chilli and caraway
Pumpkins are a good source of beta-carotene and vitamin E. They can be used in sweet or savoury dishes and are often cooked with spices. **Serves 4**

1 medium-sized butternut squash, cut into wedges
6 garlic cloves
Freshly ground black pepper
1 teaspoon thyme leaves
2 tablespoons olive oil
1 tablespoon balsamic vinegar
1 tablespoon red wine vinegar
1 tablespoon harissa
1½ teaspoons ground caraway seeds
2 tablespoons chopped coriander leaves
2 eggs, hard-boiled, peeled and quartered

Preheat the oven to 180°C/350°F/gas mark 4.

Place the squash in a roasting dish, cut side up, and add the garlic cloves. Sprinkle with pepper and half the olive oil. Roast for about 40 minutes or until soft and golden, turning from time to time. Remove from the oven and allow to cool to room temperature.

Scrape the butternut pulp from the skin and mash together with the garlic and any juices from the roasting dish. Fold in the remaining ingredients except for the eggs.

Place in a bowl and garnish with the eggs before serving.

Per serving: 157 kcals, 10g fat, 2g saturated fat, 12g carbohydrate, 0.06g sodium

Salsa verde
A light, refreshing side dish, this also makes a great accompaniment to meat dishes such as the Bacon Bollito on page 120. The pickled cucumber, lemon juice and vinegar gives this a surprising kick. **Serves 4**

1 handful flat-leaf parsley leaves
6 basil leaves
1 pickled cucumber, roughly chopped
1½ garlic cloves, roughly chopped
1 tablespoon capers, drained and rinsed
2 tinned anchovy fillets, drained and rinsed
½ tablespoon red wine vinegar
½ tablespoon lemon juice
3 tablespoons extra virgin olive oil
½ tablespoon Dijon mustard
Pinch of freshly ground black pepper

Coarsely chop together the herbs, cucumber, garlic, capers and anchovies or pulse in a food processor. (You get a better result if you hand-chop this salsa.)

Transfer the mixture to a non-reactive bowl and slowly add the remaining ingredients whilst whisking.

Per serving: 87 kcals, 9g fat, 1g saturated fat, 1g carbohydrate, 0.29g sodium

Button mushroom and baby spinach salad
A salad with attitude, one for the waistline. This light dish is perfect for summer picnics or as an accompaniment to a main course. **Serves 2**

110g (4oz) button mushrooms, cleaned and quartered
Pinch of salt
3 tablespoons lemon juice
½ teaspoon powdered rosemary
2 tablespoons roughly chopped parsley
2 teaspoons olive oil
3 tablespoons low-fat Greek yogurt
2 tablespoons skimmed milk
Freshly ground black pepper
2 handfuls baby spinach
2 tablespoons snipped chives

Place the mushrooms in a large bowl, sprinkle with a little salt and leave for 30 minutes. Rinse under cold water and dry with kitchen paper.

Combine the lemon juice, rosemary, parsley and olive oil and spoon over the mushrooms, then toss to combine.

Thin the yogurt with a little milk and pour over the mushrooms. Season with black pepper to taste.

Divide the spinach between 2 plates, spoon the mushrooms into the centre of the spinach and sprinkle with the chives.

Per serving: 75 kcals, 5g fat, 1g saturated fat, 4g carbohydrate, 0.48g sodium

Chicory salad with walnuts and croûtons

The slightly bitter taste of the chicory is offset by the nuts and sweet vinegar. Although this is relatively high in fat, most of it is unsaturated. **Serves 2**

2 heads chicory or Belgian endive
Olive-oil spray (see page 17)
1 garlic clove, diced
1 slice country bread, cut into croûtons
½ tablespoon walnut oil
4 walnuts, roughly chopped
1 tablespoon aged sherry vinegar
Freshly ground black pepper
2 tablespoons chopped chives

Separate the leaves from the chicory, and wash if necessary. Retaining a dozen larger whole leaves, shred the remainder, then set aside.

Lightly spray a frying pan with olive oil. Heat, then add the garlic and the croûtons and fry until golden. Add the shredded chicory, walnut oil and walnuts. Cook for 1 minute and then add the sherry vinegar. Season with black pepper to taste.

Arrange 6 whole chicory leaves around each plate and place the warm chicory salad in the centre. Serve immediately.

Per serving: 203 kcals, 13g fat, 1g saturated fat, 17g carbohydrate, 0.14g sodium

Seared scallops on avocado, beetroot and orange salad

Lovely colours, lovely textures and a little luxury. Choose diver-caught scallops rather than dredged as dredging damages the sea bed. **Serves 2**

Juice and grated zest of 1 orange
Juice and grated zest of 1 lime
1 tablespoon walnut oil
½ tablespoon olive oil
1 shallot, finely diced
Freshly ground black pepper
2 small cooked, but not pickled, beetroot, cut into 1cm (½in) dice
2 naval oranges, peeled, pith removed and each sliced horizontally into 5
½ avocado, peeled and diced
4 large diver-caught scallops
Olive-oil spray (see page 17)
2 teaspoons chopped dill

Whisk together the juice and zest of the orange and lime, walnut oil, the olive oil and shallot and season with black pepper to taste. Add the beetroot and leave for a couple of hours until the dressing has taken on a beautiful shade of red.

Arrange half the orange slices on each plate and scatter over the diced avocado.

Season the scallops with black pepper. Heat a non-stick frying pan over a high flame and lightly spray with olive oil. Add the scallops and cook for 1½ minutes on each side until crusty and golden, but still a little opaque in the centre. Just before serving, spoon the beetroot with its dressing over the avocado, top each plate with 2 scallops and garnish with dill.

Per serving: 270 kcals, 16g fat, 2g saturated fat, 19g carbohydrate, 0.15g sodium

Spicy sardines with chickpea and avocado salad

A great Mediterranean combo that is just as good made with tinned sardines. Sardines and chickpeas are also full of goodness. Serve as a main meal. **Serves 4**

Olive-oil spray (see page 17)

1 red chilli, diced

2 shallots, diced

1 tablespoon finely chopped flat parsley

1 tablespoon finely chopped coriander leaves

3 garlic cloves, crushed

8 sardines, scaled, cleaned, flattened out and head and backbone removed

Juice of 1 lemon

For the chickpea and avocado salad

Yolk of 1 hard-boiled egg

3 tablespoons olive oil

2 tablespoons red wine vinegar

½ red onion, finely chopped

1 garlic clove, crushed

2 tablespoons chopped flat parsley

1 tablespoon small capers, drained and rinsed

400g (14oz) tinned chickpeas, drained and rinsed

1 ripe avocado, peeled and chopped into chunky dice

Pinch of salt

Freshly ground black pepper

To make the salad, place the egg yolk in a bowl, beat in the oil and vinegar and stir in the onion, garlic, parsley, capers, chickpeas and avocado. Season with salt and black pepper to taste.

Preheat the oven to 180°C/350°F/gas mark 4.

Lightly spray a small frying pan with olive-oil spray, then add the chilli and shallots and cook until softened but not coloured. Fold in the parsley, coriander and garlic and season with black pepper, then spread over the flesh side of the fish.

Roll up the sardines and secure with 2 small wooden cocktail sticks that have been soaked in water. Cook in the oven for 5–8 minutes, then place the sardines on a plate and drizzle with lemon juice.

To serve, place a pile of salad on to each serving plate and top with two sardine rolls.

Per serving: 407 kcals, 28g fat, 4g saturated fat, 13g carbohydrate, 0.45g sodium

Mediterranean seafood salad

A special balance of flavours in a healthy package. The Mediterranean diet is one of the healthiest in the world, with its combination of fresh fish, olive oil and colourful vegetables. **Serves 6**

125ml (4fl oz) dry white wine

1kg (2¼lb) mussels, cleaned

6 squid tubes, cut into rings

18 raw tiger prawns, peeled

6 diver-caught scallops, halved

175g (6oz) tinned cockles or baby clams, shelled and drained

125g (4½oz) cooked white crab meat

3 garlic cloves, crushed

2 red chillies, finely sliced

½ red onion, diced

3 tablespoons olive oil

1 tablespoon lemon juice

Freshly ground black pepper

2 tablespoons chopped parsley

Crisp lettuce

In a large saucepan, bring the white wine to the boil, add the mussels, cover and cook for 5 minutes or until the mussels have opened. Remove the mussels from the pan and set aside, reserving the liquid. Discard any that remain closed. Shell the mussels when cool enough to handle.

In the boiling juices that remain in the pan, cook the squid, prawns and scallops for 1 minute. Remove (do not throw away the cooking liquid), allow the shellfish to cool and combine with the mussels, cockles or clams and white crab meat.

Boil the mussel cooking liquid until it has reduced to about 4 tablespoons. Combine with the garlic, chillies, onion, olive oil and lemon juice. Pour the juices over the seafood and toss to combine. Refrigerate for 30 minutes, season with black pepper and fold in the chopped parsley.

Serve on a bed of crisp lettuce with some warm crusty wholegrain bread to mop up the juices.

Per serving: 243 kcals, 9g fat, 1g saturated fat, 4g carbohydrate, 0.46g sodium

A warm salad of asparagus, field mushrooms and fresh peas

Something a little different, this is a wonderful spring dish, when asparagus and fresh peas are in season. **Serves 2**

10 medium asparagus spears, trimmed and peeled if necessary

75g (3oz) podded young peas

2 tablespoons olive oil

1 garlic clove, mashed to a paste

4 field mushrooms, stalks removed, peeled if necessary

Freshly ground black pepper

2 slices wholemeal bread

½ shallot, finely chopped

3 tablespoons dry Martini (optional)

2 tablespoons low-fat yogurt

½ tablespoon chopped flat parsley

½ tablespoon snipped chives

½ teaspoon chopped tarragon

½ tablespoon lemon juice

½ handful rocket

½ handful watercress

Cook the asparagus in boiling water for 1 minute, drain, reserving the cooking water, and set aside.

Add the peas to the asparagus cooking water and cook for 2 minutes, drain, then set aside.

Prepare your barbecue, grill or griddle pan.

Combine the olive oil and garlic and brush over the asparagus and the mushrooms. Season the asparagus and mushrooms with black pepper.

Grill or barbecue the mushrooms for 5 minutes on each side and the asparagus for 2 minutes each side. Keep both warm. Brush the both sides of the bread with garlic-infused oil and grill until both sides are toasted.

In a saucepan, heat the remaining garlic oil, add the shallot, and over a medium heat allow to cook without colouring. Add the dry Martini, if using, increase the heat and cook for a further minute. Remove the pan from the heat and whisk in the yogurt a little at a time. Fold in the peas, parsley, chives, tarragon and lemon juice. Season to taste. Return to a gentle heat to warm through.

Combine the rocket and watercress and divide between 2 plates. Top the leaves with a slice of the grilled bread. Divide the asparagus and mushrooms between the bread slices, arranging them attractively on top of each slice. Spoon the peas and juices over the salad leaves.

Per serving: 261 kcals, 14g fat, 2g saturated fat, 24g carbohydrate, 0.22g sodium

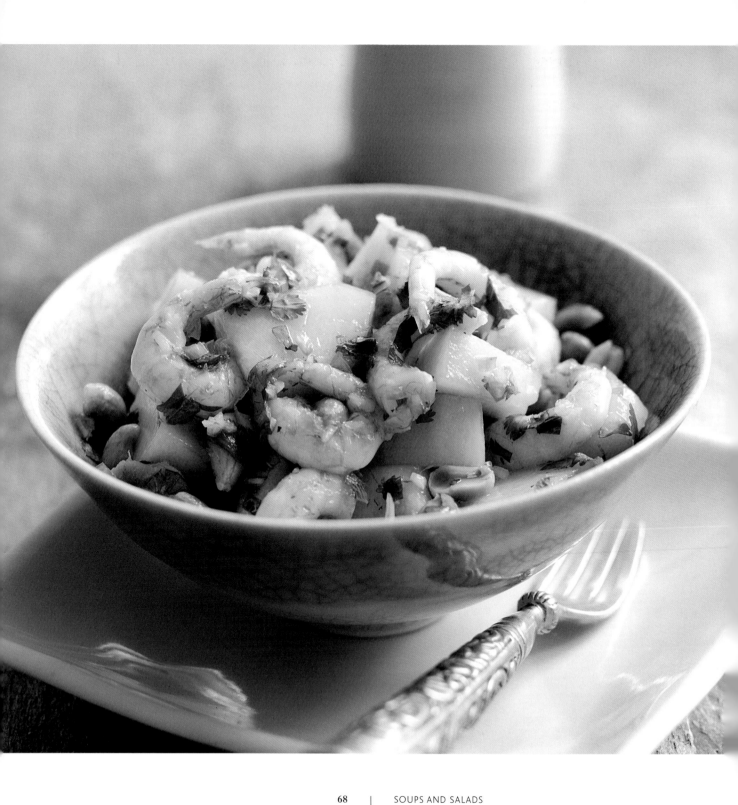

Thai-inspired melon salad
This salad was created as a result of my visits to Thailand. Their vibrant flavours go well with melon, creating a refreshing salad with a twist. As this is a salty salad, keep the rest of the day's intake low. **Serves 4**

2 garlic cloves, crushed
1 tablespoon liquid honey
2 teaspoons nam pla (Thai fish sauce)
Juice of 2 limes
1 tablespoon grated lime zest
2 red chillies, finely diced
175g (6oz) cooked and shelled shrimp or prawns
50g (2oz) unsalted roasted peanuts
1 Galia or Ogen melon, peeled and chopped into 2.5cm (1in) dice
4 tablespoons chopped coriander leaves
1 tablespoon chopped mint leaves

In a large bowl, combine the garlic, honey, nam pla, lime juice, lime zest and chillies. Fold in the shrimp and peanuts. Add the melon and stir to combine.
Garnish with chopped coriander and mint. Chill until ready to serve.

Per serving: 162 kcals, 7g fat, 1g saturated fat, 10g carbohydrate, 1.87g sodium

Prawn and sweetcorn salad
This is the salad for those in a hurry. Just chuck it all together in a bowl to create a healthy meal in minutes. Quick, simple and exceedingly tasty. **Serves 2**

1 egg yolk
2 tablespoons olive oil
1 tablespoon lemon juice
½ tablespoon Dijon mustard
2 tablespoons low-fat Greek yogurt
2 tablespoons snipped chives
2 tablespoons snipped dill
1 tablespoon sliced spring onion
12 frozen prawns, cooked
175g (6oz) fresh or frozen sweetcorn kernels, cooked

Whisk together the egg yolk, oil, lemon juice and mustard. Once this has emulsified, fold in the yogurt.
Add the herbs and spring onion and combine with the prawns and sweetcorn.

Per serving: 426 kcals, 19g fat, 3g saturated fat, 18g carbohydrate, 1.57g sodium

Rare tuna salade niçoise

This was inspired by the classic salade niçoise, which uses tinned tuna. Fresh tuna, of course, contains lots of beneficial omega-3 fatty oils. Eat as a main course with crusty bread. **Serves 2**

2 x 100g (3½oz) fresh tuna steaks, each ideally 2.5cm (1in) thick

4 new salad potatoes

2 eggs, at room temperature

50g (2oz) extra-fine French beans, trimmed

2 Little Gem lettuce hearts, quartered lengthways and separated into leaves

2 plum tomatoes, roughly chopped

½ red onion, finely sliced

4 tinned anchovy fillets, drained, rinsed and cut lengthways into thin strips

10 black olives, pitted

8 basil leaves, torn

For the marinade

2 tablespoons olive oil

1 tablespoon aged red wine vinegar

1 tablespoon chopped flat parsley

1 tablespoon snipped chives

1 garlic clove, finely chopped

Freshly ground black pepper

To make the marinade, place the olive oil, vinegar, parsley, chives, garlic and a teaspoon of pepper in a bowl, whisking to combine.

Place the tuna in a shallow non-metallic dish and pour over half of the marinade. Cover with clingfilm and chill for 1 hour to allow the flavours to penetrate the tuna, turning after about 30 minutes or so.

Place the potatoes in a pan of boiling water, cover and simmer for 10–12 minutes or until just tender. Drain, then cut into quarters lengthways.

Place the eggs in a small pan and just cover with boiling water, then cook for 6 minutes. Drain and rinse under cold running water, remove the shells and cut each egg in half; they should still be slightly soft. Plunge the French beans in a pan of boiling water and blanch for 3 minutes or so, then drain and refresh in cold water.

Heat a griddle pan for 5 minutes. Remove the tuna from the marinade, shaking off any excess. Cook the tuna for about 2 minutes on each side, depending on how rare you like it.

Arrange the lettuce leaves on serving plates or on 1 large platter and add the potatoes, French beans, tomatoes, onion and anchovies. Place the tuna steaks on top and drizzle over the remaining marinade. Scatter over the eggs, olives and torn basil leaves to serve.

Per serving: 442 kcals, 25g fat, 5g saturated fat, 21g carbohydrate, 0.71g sodium

Asian chicken salad

With the great flavours of the Orient — papaya, coriander, mint, chilli and lime — this is a simple salad to make, but full of flavour. Perfect for a light lunch or as an appetiser. **Serves 4**

450g (1lb) shredded chicken from 'The Really Useful Chicken' recipe (see page 116)

1 carrot, cut into julienne

½ green paw-paw or papaya, peeled and cut into julienne

3 tablespoons chopped mint

3 tablespoons chopped coriander leaves

1 bunch spring onions, sliced

½ celeriac, cut into julienne

25g (1oz) unsalted peanuts, roughly chopped

Freshly ground black pepper

For the dressing

2 teaspoons finely chopped garlic

1 tablespoon finely chopped chilli

150ml (5fl oz) lime juice

2 tablespoons nam pla (Thai fish sauce) or reduced-salt light soy sauce

1 tablespoon liquid honey

To make the dressing, combine the ingredients in a bowl.
In another large bowl, mix the remaining ingredients with enough of the dressing to coat and season well with black pepper to taste.

Per serving: 297 kcals, 12g fat, 3g saturated fat, 12g carbohydrate, 0.69g sodium

Asian slaw

A healthier alternative to normal mayonnaise-based coleslaw, this recipe again draws on the delicious tastes of the Far East, where the diet is low in saturated fat that the Western world would do well to follow. **Serves 2**

225g (8oz) pak choi, shredded

125g (4½oz) carrots, cut into julienne

4 shallots, sliced

½ tablespoon grated fresh root ginger

2 tablespoons shredded basil leaves

2 tablespoons coriander leaves

1 tablespoon mint leaves

1 garlic clove, chopped

1 hot chilli, seeded and finely chopped

Juice and grated zest of 1 orange

Juice of 2 limes

1 tablespoon nam pla (Thai fish sauce)

½ teaspoon sugar

2 tablespoons groundnut oil

Freshly ground black pepper

1 tablespoon crushed roasted peanuts

Mix the pak choi in a bowl with the carrots, shallots, ginger, basil, coriander, mint, garlic, chilli and orange zest.
In a small bowl, whisk together the orange juice, lime juice, nam pla and sugar. Slowly whisk in the oil until emulsified. Add the dressing to the pak choi and toss well. Season with pepper. Cover and chill for 2–6 hours.
Just before serving, sprinkle with the crushed roasted peanuts.

Per serving: 222 kcals, 16g fat, 3g saturated fat, 16g carbohydrate, 0.82g sodium

Light Meals and Appetisers

3

Mushroom 'caviar' *An excellent alternative to the usual range of dips, and much healthier. Although the texture may resemble caviar, it has nothing to do with fish or fish roe.*

Serves 4

1 tablespoon olive oil
½ onion, finely diced
2 garlic cloves, finely diced
1 teaspoon thyme leaves

110g (4oz) field mushrooms, roughly chopped
1 tablespoon balsamic vinegar
Freshly ground black pepper

Heat the oil in a deep saucepan over a medium heat. Add the onion, garlic and thyme and cook until soft but not brown. **Add** the mushrooms, stir to combine, and increase the heat. Cook for 10 minutes, or until the mushrooms have released their liquid. Then add the balsamic vinegar and cook until all the liquid has evaporated. Season with black pepper to taste.
Blend the mixture in a food processor until roughly chopped but not pulverised. Serve warm or at room temperature with crusty wholegrain bread or oatcakes.

Per serving: 39 kcals, 3g fat, 0.4g saturated fat, 3g carbohydrate, 0g sodium

Asparagus with red pepper sauce
The red peppers add a natural sweetness to the asparagus, a great partnership and fantastic combination of colours. Eat as an appetiser or to accompany a main course. Serves 4

2 red peppers, seeded and roughly chopped
1 onion, roughly chopped
2 garlic cloves, crushed
1 red chilli, finely diced
12 basil leaves, plus extra to garnish

1 tablespoon walnut oil
1 tablespoon sherry vinegar
2 tablespoons lemon juice
310g (11oz) asparagus, trimmed
Freshly ground black pepper

Place all the ingredients except the asparagus in a large, non-reactive (not aluminium) saucepan, cover and simmer gently for 20 minutes, stirring from time to time.
Pour the softened pepper mix into a food processor and blend until smooth. Pass through a fine sieve and set aside, keeping it warm, if you wish.
Cook the asparagus in boiling water for 6 minutes, then drain.
Spoon the red pepper sauce (hot or cold) on to 4 plates and top with the asparagus. Garnish with basil leaves and ground black pepper.

Per serving: 79 kcals, 4g fat, 0.3g saturated fat, 9g carbohydrate, 0.01g sodium

Bruschetta with white bean purée and raw mushrooms
A much healthier version of a classic dish, this has lots of fibre and even more flavour.

Serves 4

2 tablespoons olive oil	Freshly ground black pepper
2 garlic cloves, 1 of them finely diced, 1 halved	50g (2oz) button mushrooms, cleaned and sliced
1 teaspoon finely chopped rosemary leaves	Juice of ½ lemon
425g (15oz) tinned cannellini beans, rinsed and drained	1 tablespoon chopped oregano leaves
150ml (5fl oz) vegetable stock	4 thick slices wholegrain country bread

In a saucepan, combine 1 tablespoon of the olive oil, the diced garlic and the rosemary and cook over a gentle heat until the garlic is soft but without colour.

Add the beans and stock, stir to combine, then cook for about 10 minutes. If the mixture dries out too much, add a little more vegetable stock to moisten. Mash with a potato masher or pulse in a food processor to create a rough purée. Season to taste with ground black pepper.

Meanwhile toss the sliced mushrooms with the remaining olive oil, the lemon juice, oregano and some black pepper.

Grill the bread on both sides and rub with the halved garlic clove. Top with the bean purée, then the mushroom mix. Serve with some salad leaves.

Per serving: 225 kcals, 7g fat, 1g saturated fat, 32g carbohydrate, 0.36g sodium

Stewed artichokes with spices and apricots and other things

A wonderfully spicy, nutritious vegetarian stew that is well worth the effort.

Serves 4

4 large globe artichokes

Juice of 1 lemon, lemon peel reserved

2 garlic cloves, finely sliced

10 black peppercorns

12 coriander seeds, toasted

½ teaspoon ground turmeric

⅛ teaspoon cayenne pepper

½ teaspoon cumin seeds, toasted

2 onions, cut in eighths

2 bay leaves

50ml (2fl oz) olive oil

Pinch of saffron strands, soaked in a little cold water

2 carrots, sliced

600ml (1 pint) vegetable stock

8 dried apricots, sliced

50g (2oz) raisins

25g (1oz) almonds, sliced

400g (14oz) tinned chickpeas, drained and rinsed

225g (8oz) baby spinach

2 tablespoons roughly chopped coriander leaves

4 tablespoons roughly chopped flat parsley

Trim the artichokes by peeling the stem until all woody matter has disappeared. Pull off all the tough outer leaves until you reach the pale green ones. Cut off about 2.5cm (1in) from the top of the artichoke. Cut the artichoke vertically into 4 and cut or pull out the choke. Rub all the cut surfaces with the lemon peel and place the artichoke quarters in a bowl of water. Add the lemon juice.

Using a mortar and pestle or coffee grinder, crush the garlic, peppercorns, coriander seeds, turmeric, cayenne and cumin seeds.

In a saucepan, cook the onions and bay leaves in the olive oil over a medium heat until they have softened but not coloured, this should take about 8 minutes. Add the spice mix and cook for a further 3 minutes.

Add the drained artichokes and the saffron with its soaking liquor and toss to combine. Add the carrots, half the vegetable stock, the apricots, raisins and almonds and simmer, covered for about 20 minutes, stirring from time to time. Add more stock as necessary.

When the artichokes are tender, add the chickpeas, spinach, coriander leaves and parsley and stir to combine. Cook until the spinach has wilted. Season with black pepper to taste.

Serve hot or cold with steamed couscous.

Per serving: 416 kcals, 19g fat, 2g saturated fat, 46g carbohydrate, 0.52g sodium

Stuffed peppers with brandade

A French dish, brandade is made by beating milk, olive oil and poached fish into a paste. Usually made with salt cod, it works equally well with fresh cod or haddock. **Serves 4**

2 potatoes, cut into 2.5cm (1in) cubes
350g (12oz) fresh cod
150ml (5fl oz) semi-skimmed milk
2 garlic cloves, crushed
Juice of 1 lemon

2 tablespoons olive oil
50g (2oz) ground almonds (optional)
Freshly ground black pepper
4 drained wood-roasted peppers
Lemon wedges, to serve

Cook the potatoes in water until soft. Mash and set aside.

Place the cod in a shallow frying pan, add the milk and bring to the boil. Remove from the heat and allow the cod to cool in the milk.

When the cod is cool enough to handle, remove from the milk and flake into a large bowl. Add the garlic, lemon juice, olive oil and almonds (if using) and combine well. Add the mashed potato to make a fairly thick paste. Season with black pepper to taste.

Stuff each pepper with the brandade paste and serve at room temperature, garnished with lemon wedges.

Per serving: 332 kcals, 20g fat, 3g saturated fat, 19g carbohydrate, 1.28g sodium

Tortino
This is similar to a frittata *or* tortilla *in that the eggs hold the asparagus and spinach together to make a vegetarian 'cake' (colloquially,* tortino *means cake in Italian). Great for a light meal.* **Serves 4**

225g (8oz) asparagus, cut into 2.5cm (1in) pieces
1 shallot, finely diced
10g (½oz) unsalted butter
2 handfuls spinach, thick stems removed

1 teaspoon soft thyme leaves
5 large eggs, beaten
1 tablespoon skimmed milk
1 tablespoon grated Parmesan, cheese
Freshly ground black pepper

Preheat the oven to 200°C/400°F/gas mark 6.

Blanch the asparagus in boiling water for 3 minutes, then refresh in cold water to arrest the cooking. Drain.

Pan-fry the shallot in the butter until softened but not coloured, then add the spinach and thyme leaves and cook until the leaves have wilted. Squeeze the liquid from the spinach and transfer the drained mix to a lightly buttered shallow baking dish. Place the asparagus over the spinach.

Beat the eggs, then combine with the milk and Parmesan. Season with black pepper and pour over the vegetables. Lift the vegetables slightly to allow the egg to cover the bottom of the dish.

Place in the oven and cook for about 15 minutes or until the eggs are set. This dish can be eaten hot or at room temperature.

Per serving: 162 kcals, 12g fat, 4g saturated fat, 2g carbohydrate, 0.16g sodium

Oriental smoked salmon rolls

Canapés, snacks, brunch — this is perfect for all kinds of occasions. Make sure that the fresh colours of the radish, paw-paw and cucumber peek out from the salmon rolls. **Makes 24 rolls**

1 green paw-paw or papaya, peeled and cut into thin matchsticks

½ cucumber, peeled and cut into thin matchsticks

8 radishes, thinly sliced

125ml (4fl oz) rice wine vinegar

Juice and zest of 3 limes

1 tablespoon reduced-salt soy sauce

1 tablespoon liquid honey

6 spring onions, finely shredded

350g (12oz) smoked salmon, cut into long strips

48 mint leaves

48 coriander leaves

Combine the papaya, cucumber and radishes in a bowl.

Whisk together the rice wine vinegar, lime juice and zest, soy sauce and the honey, then pour over the papaya salad and allow to stand for 2 hours. Drain and fold in the spring onions.

Cut the smoked salmon in 7.5cm (3in) lengths. Place 2 leaves of each herb on the salmon, top with a little of the pickled vegetables and roll up tightly. Cover and refrigerate until ready to serve.

Per roll: 28 kcals, 0.7g fat, 0.1g saturated fat, 2g carbohydrate, 0.3g sodium

Salmon and haddock fishcakes

Everybody loves fishcakes and these are particularly good ones, great hot or cold. Serve with the Salsa Verde on page 62.

Serves 4

275 g (10oz) smoked haddock fillets

175g (6oz) salmon fillets

600ml (1 pint) skimmed milk

1 onion, sliced

1 carrot, chopped

1 bay leaf

1 teaspoon black peppercorns

2 cloves

2 tablespoons olive oil

2 eggs

275g (10oz) potatoes, cooked and mashed

2 teaspoons anchovy essence

2 eggs, hard-boiled, peeled and chopped

2 tablespoons chopped parsley

1 tablespoon chopped dill

Freshly ground black pepper

Plain flour

Fresh wholegrain breadcrumbs

Place the haddock and salmon in a large frying-pan or roasting pan. Add enough milk to cover. Add one-third of the onion, the carrot, bay leaf, peppercorns and cloves. Bring to the boil and then simmer for 6 minutes. Set aside to cool slightly.

Cut the rest of the onion into dice. Heat half of the olive oil in a pan and briefly sweat the onion until softened, this should take about 6–8 minutes.

Remove the fish from the milk and flake the fish, discarding any skin or bones. Strain the liquid and reserve.

Beat 1 of the eggs. Combine the haddock with the mashed potato, sweated onions, beaten egg and anchovy essence. Fold in the hard-boiled eggs, parsley and dill until well combined, but do not over-mix. Season with black pepper to taste. If the mixture is too dry, mix in some of the strained fish liquid.

Divide the mixture into four, and shape into patties.

Beat the remaining egg with a little water in a bowl. Season the flour and place on a plate. Place the breadcrumbs on another plate. Dip the patties in the flour, the egg and finally the breadcrumbs. Refrigerate for 2 hours.

Pan-fry the fishcakes in the remaining olive oil for 5 minutes on each side, and keep warm in the oven.

Per serving: 424 kcals, 20g fat, 5g saturated fat, 28g carbohydrate, 0.91g sodium

Stuffed sardines
This sardine dish has a hint of Moroccan influence, with its filling of nuts and currants. Sardines are a great-tasting oily fish, full of healthy omega-3 fatty acids.

Serves 4 as a starter (2 as a main course)

1 red onion, very finely
  chopped
3 tablespoons olive oil
30g (1¼ oz) fresh wholegrain
  breadcrumbs
5 tablespoons currants, soaked
  in water for 15 minutes if
  very dry
3 tablespoons pine kernels
1 bunch parsley, chopped
5 tablespoons mixed lemon
  and orange juice

Freshly ground black pepper
Olive-oil spray (see page 17)
12 sardines, scaled, cleaned,
  flattened out and head and
  backbone removed
½ lemon, cut into 5mm (¼in)
  thick slices
½ orange, cut into 5mm (¼in)
  thick slices
12 fresh or 6 dried bay leaves,
  broken in half

In a saucepan, sweat the onion in the olive oil. Add the breadcrumbs and cook for 2–3 minutes. Remove from the heat and add the currants, pine nuts and parsley. Pour in the citrus juices and stir. Season with black pepper and mix well. Allow to cool.

Preheat the oven to 200°C/400°F/gas mark 6.

Lightly oil a baking dish with the olive-oil spray. Fill each sardine with 1–2 teaspoons of filling. Roll each fish from head to tail. Pack the sardines tightly together in the dish with their tails sticking up in the same direction. Sprinkle them with the remaining filling. Place the orange and lemon slices and the bay leaves around the dish and tucked between the sardines. Bake for 10–15 minutes or until golden.

Serve warm or at room temperature.

Per serving: 489 kcals, 29g fat, 5g saturated fat, 25g carbohydrate, 0.23g sodium

Creamy sardines on toast
Sardines on toast never tasted so good. Tinned sardines also contain omega-3 fats and are really versatile store-cupboard food. A great snack.

Serves 2

1 tablespoon olive oil
½ onion, finely diced
1 teaspoon soft thyme leaves
3 tablespoons wholemeal
  breadcrumbs
150ml (5fl oz) low-fat yogurt

1 small tin sardines, drained
  and mashed
2 eggs, hard-boiled, peeled and
  chopped
Freshly ground black pepper
2 slices wholegrain bread

Heat the olive oil in a frying pan, add the onion and thyme and cook until the onion is soft but not brown. Add the remaining ingredients except the bread and warm through, stirring to combine. Season with black pepper to taste.

Preheat the grill. Toast the bread, then share the mixture equally between the slices. Pop under a hot grill until the mixture bubbles. Serve hot.

Per serving: 442 kcals, 23g fat, 5g saturated fat, 29g carbohydrate, 0.73g sodium

A bowl of steaming mussels

Mussels are such good value and this recipe is a variation on the traditional French dish, Moules marinière. **Serves 4 as a starter (2 as a main course)**

1 tablespoon olive oil	1 glass white wine
1 onion, finely diced	150ml (5fl oz) fish stock
4 tinned anchovy fillets, drained, rinsed and chopped	1kg (2¼lb) mussels, cleaned
4 large garlic cloves, chopped	4 tablespoons finely chopped parsley
1 red chilli, chopped	Freshly ground black pepper

Heat the olive oil in a large saucepan over a medium heat. Add the onion, anchovies, garlic and chilli and cook until the onion is soft but not brown. Add the wine and the stock and bring to the boil. Simmer for 5 minutes, then add the mussels and cover. Increase the heat and cook for approximately 5 minutes, shaking the pan from time to time.

Remove the mussels with a slotted spoon to warm bowls, discarding any that have not opened.

Boil the remaining liquid for a further 2 minutes, then add the parsley and season with ground black pepper. Pour over the mussels and serve with crusty wholegrain bread.

Per serving: 130 kcals, 5g fat, 1g saturated fat, 6g carbohydrate, 0.39g sodium

Sardines with tomatoes and red onion

Another great sardine recipe, this makes a delicious light lunch or supper, simple to prepare with ingredients that you will probably have in your cupboard. **Serves 4**

500g (1lb 2oz) fresh plum tomatoes, sliced	Pinch of dried red chilli flakes
½ red onion, finely sliced	Freshly ground black pepper
2 tins of sardines, drained and rinsed	Balsamic vinegar, to taste
3 pinches of dried oregano	Fresh marjoram leaves
	Handful of black olives

Arrange the tomato slices on a serving plate so that they overlap. Scatter with red onion slices. Arrange the sardines carefully over the tomatoes. Sprinkle the sardines with oregano, chilli flakes and freshly ground black pepper.

Drizzle a little balsamic vinegar over the plate. Garnish with some fresh marjoram leaves and black olives. Serve at room temperature.

Per serving: 192 kcals, 11g fat, 2g saturated fat, 6g carbohydrate, 0.47g sodium

Tuna kebabs with pickled lemon and mint
Great for a barbecue, these kebabs are both tasty and nutritious. Tuna and tomatoes are Mediterranean 'musts', especially when combined with sunshine! **Serves 4**

4 pickled lemons

1 bunch mint, leaves only

4 garlic cloves, roughly chopped

½ teaspoon dried red chilli flakes

1 tablespoon olive oil

1kg (2¼lb) tuna loin, cut into 16 even-sized cubes

12 bay leaves

12 cherry tomatoes

Cut the pickled lemons in half, scoop out the flesh and discard. Cut the rinds of 3 of the lemons into 12 pieces of roughly even size. Place the rind of the fourth lemon in a food processor with the mint, garlic, chilli flakes, oil and 2 tablespoons of water and pulse until smooth. Spoon into a bowl, then add the tuna pieces and marinate for 20 minutes.

Slide 1 piece of tuna on to a bamboo skewer that has been soaked in water. Follow the tuna with 1 bay leaf, 1 tomato and 1 piece of lemon rind. Do this three more times, finishing the kebab with a piece of tuna. Prepare three more skewers in this way.

Preheat the grill to its highest setting or heat a large frying pan or griddle pan. Char-grill the skewers for 1 minute on each side until they are medium rare, or as you like them. Serve with a leaf salad.

Per serving: 393 kcals, 15g fat, 4g saturated fat, 5g carbohydrate, 0.52g sodium

Anchovy toasts
An unusual dish, but it's worth being a little avant-garde for these delicious flavours. Anchovies are usually bought tinned, but fresh anchovies are a delicacy in Portugal, Spain and Turkey. **Serves 4 (2 as a main course)**

4 dried figs, roughly chopped

1 tablespoon Pernod

4 tablespoons green tea

50g (2oz) whole almonds, toasted

25g (1oz) macadamia nuts

4 spring onions, roughly chopped

2 garlic cloves, roughly chopped

1 teaspoon tarragon leaves

1 teaspoon dill leaves

1 teaspoon flat-leaf parsley

2 sun-dried tomatoes, drained

3 cherry peppers, seeded

Juice and zest of 2 limes

1 tablespoon olive oil

4 slices wholegrain bread, toasted

8 tinned anchovy fillets, drained, rinsed and sliced in half lengthways

Preheat the oven to 200°C/400°F/gas mark 6.

Soak the figs in the Pernod and tea for 2 hours. Combine the figs with the remaining ingredients except the toast and anchovies.

Spread the fig mixture on the toast and cook in the oven for 10 minutes. Cut each slice into 2 pieces and top with the anchovy fillets. Eat while hot.

Per serving: 315 kcals, 18g fat, 2g saturated fat, 30g carbohydrate, 0.5g sodium

Trout in a red pepper blanket

Trout is such an underrated fish, but it is excellent value, great tasting and high in omega-3. Together with red peppers and garlic, this is an unbeatable combination. **Serves 4**

3 red peppers, seeded and quartered
50g (2oz) pine kernels, toasted
50g (2oz) fresh breadcrumbs
3 garlic cloves, finely chopped
Olive-oil spray (see page 17)
Freshly ground black pepper
4 'spatchcocked' trout (ask your fishmonger to open and fillet the trout, removing the head and tail)

Char the peppers in the oven or over a gas flame until the skin is blackened. Place the peppers in a paper bag and seal. Allow the peppers to steam in their own heat for 15 minutes, then remove and peel. Place in a food processor with their juice and blend.

Add the pine kernels, breadcrumbs and garlic and blend again to a smooth purée. With the food processor running, add the olive oil in a thin stream. Season with black pepper to taste.

Rub the trout on both sides with the red pepper purée. Refrigerate for 30 minutes.

Heat a ridged griddle plate, large frying-pan or barbecue until very hot. Lightly spray the surface with olive oil and cook the trout, flesh-side down, for 3 minutes. Turn the fish carefully and cook for a further 3 minutes.

Transfer to a serving platter and serve with noodles, rice or new potatoes.

Per serving: 369 kcals, 16g fat, 3g saturated fat, 18g carbohydrate, 0.2g sodium

Chilli-corn crabcakes

Crabcakes are an all-time favourite of mine and these can be made the day before and stored in the fridge. White crab meat comes from the claw, the brown meat from the body. Serve with a green salad. **Serves 6**

450g (1lb) white crab meat, picked over
225g (8oz) brown crab meat
1 chilli, finely diced
1 onion, finely diced
½ red pepper, seeded and finely diced
2 celery sticks, finely diced
200g (7oz) tinned sweetcorn, drained
2 teaspoons chopped dill
150ml (5fl oz) low-fat Greek yogurt
1 teaspoon mustard powder
2 eggs, lightly beaten
50g (2oz) fresh wholemeal breadcrumbs
3 tablespoons rapeseed oil
Freshly ground black pepper

In a large bowl, mix together the white and brown crab meat, chilli, onion, red pepper, celery, sweetcorn and dill.

Combine the yogurt, mustard powder and eggs in another bowl and then slowly add half the oil. Add the crab mixture and mix well. Fold in a third of the breadcrumbs, or as much as you need to firm the mixture, and season to taste with black pepper. Refrigerate for 2 hours ideally.

Make the mixture into 6 large or 12 small patties. Coat each one in the remaining breadcrumbs. These cakes can be made well ahead of when they are needed; at this point put them in the fridge to dry out overnight.

Heat the remaining oil in a large pan over a medium heat, and cook the cakes for 3 minutes on each side. Serve hot.

Per serving: 306 kcals, 16g fat, 3g saturated fat, 14g carbohydrate, 0.64g sodium

Chicken liver pâté
The easiest pâté I know, this takes just minutes to prepare. Eat hot or cold, with pickles, Melba toast or crusty wholegrain bread, this is a great snack or lunch.

Serves 4

Rapeseed-oil spray (see page 17)
225g (8oz) chicken livers, cleaned
300ml (10fl oz) skimmed milk
3 egg yolks

1 shallot, finely diced
1 garlic clove, finely diced
1 teaspoon soft thyme leaves
Freshly ground black pepper
25g (1oz) fresh breadcrumbs

Preheat the oven to 160°C/325°F/gas mark 3.

Lightly spray 4 small moulds or ramekins with oil.

Put the livers, milk, egg yolks, shallot, garlic and thyme in a food processor and blend until smooth. Season with black pepper.

Pass through a fine sieve and then fold in the breadcrumbs.

Spoon the mixture into the moulds and then place in a roasting tray. Add hot water to the tray until it comes three-quarters of way up the sides of the moulds. Cook in the oven until the pâté has set, this should take about 20 minutes.

Per serving: 150 kcals, 6g fat, 2g saturated fat, 9g carbohydrate, 0.14g sodium

Chicken stir-fry with black beans
Chinese food offers lots of flavours, but very little fat. In fact, along with the Mediterranean diet, it is one we could learn a few tips from. **Serves 2**

Y = NOT FOLLOWED

1 egg white
3 teaspoons cornflour
2 skinless chicken breasts, cut into thin strips
X ½ tablespoon groundnut oil
2 garlic cloves, finely chopped
2.5cm (1in) fresh root ginger, peeled and grated
Pinch of dried red chilli flakes
1 tablespoon Chinese black beans, finely chopped
X 1 carrot, sliced on the diagonal

½ red pepper, seeded and cut into diamonds
½ yellow pepper, seeded and cut into diamonds
125 ml (4½fl oz) chicken stock
1 tablespoon reduced-salt dark soy sauce
2 tablespoons rice wine vinegar
Y Pinch of sugar
75g (3oz) sugar-snap peas
4 spring onions, sliced on the diagonal

+ BOK CHOI + MUSHROOMS + CHERRY TOMATOE

Lightly beat the egg white in a non-metallic bowl with half the cornflour. Add the chicken, cover with clingfilm and chill for 30 minutes (this is called velveting).

X **Place** 300ml (10fl oz) water in a pan and bring to the boil. Stir the chicken and then remove from the bowl with a slotted spoon. Remove the pan from the heat and add the chicken, stirring to prevent it from sticking together, then return to the heat and cook for 1½ minutes or until the chicken is white and just tender. Drain on kitchen paper.

Heat a wok and swirl in the oil. Add the garlic, ginger, chilli flakes and black beans and stir-fry for 15 seconds, then add the carrot and stir-fry for 1 minute. Stir in the cooked chicken and the peppers. Pour in the stock, then add the soy sauce, vinegar and sugar, stirring to combine.

Increase the heat and bring to the boil, then reduce to a simmer. Add the sugar-snap peas and spring onions and cook for 2 minutes. Mix the remaining cornflour with 1 tablespoon water and stir into the wok. Cook for a minute or so until the sauce clears and thickens.

Serve at once in Chinese-style bowls with steamed rice.

Per serving: 289 kcals, 5g fat, 1g saturated fat, 22g carbohydrate, 0.95g sodium

Hot chilli chicken fajitas

Mexico in its most popular foodie form. The cool flavours of the salsa take the edge of the hot chicken marinade and it needs no further accompaniment. Cook on the barbecue or a griddle pan. **Serves 4**

1 tablespoon chilli oil
1 tablespoon hot chilli powder
1 tablespoon paprika
Pinch of caster sugar
Grated zest and juice of 1 lime
2 skinless chicken breast fillets
4 soft flour tortillas
¼ small iceberg lettuce, shredded
75ml (3fl oz) low-fat yogurt

For the tomato and avocado salsa
2 large tomatoes, seeded and finely diced
1 red chilli, seeded and finely chopped
Juice of 1 lime
½ small red onion, finely chopped
1 ripe avocado, peeled, stoned and finely diced
1 tablespoon olive oil
8 tablespoons roughly chopped coriander leaves
Freshly ground black pepper

Soak eight 15cm (6in) bamboo skewers in water overnight.
Mix together the chilli oil, chilli powder, paprika, sugar and the lime zest and juice in a shallow non-metallic dish.
Cut each chicken breast lengthways into 6 strips. Add to the chilli mixture and stir until well coated, then cover with clingfilm and leave to marinate in the fridge for 1–2 hours.
To make the tomato and avocado salsa, place all the ingredients into a large bowl and stir gently to combine. Season with black pepper to taste and spoon into a serving bowl. Cover with clingfilm and set aside to allow the flavours to develop, but don't make this too far in advance otherwise the avocado may blacken.

Heat a griddle pan or a barbecue. Thread 3 pieces of chicken on to each soaked bamboo skewer and place on the griddle pan or barbecue. Cook for 3–4 minutes on each side or until the chicken is cooked through and lightly charred.
Heat a frying or griddle pan. Add a tortilla and heat for 30 seconds, or until soft and pliable, turning once. Repeat with the remaining tortillas and stack up on a warmed plate. Place the chicken skewers on a serving platter and hand around the tomato and avocado salsa, warmed tortillas, lettuce and yogurt, allowing each person to assemble the fajitas themselves.

Per serving: 392 kcals, 15g fat, 2g saturated fat, 42g carbohydrate, 0.27g sodium

Souvlakia

Memories of Greek holidays, hot sun, white sands and warm seas. This Mediterranean staple makes a simple but filling meal, great also for packed lunches and picnics.

Serves 2

225g (8oz) lamb fillets, cut into 1cm (½in) slices
½ onion, grated
3 garlic cloves, mashed to a paste with a little salt
1 teaspoon freshly ground black pepper
1 teaspoon ground cumin
½ teaspoon cayenne pepper
2 tablespoons olive oil
2 wholemeal pitta breads
Juice of ½ lemon
4 tablespoons low-fat yogurt
½ teaspoon chopped mint leaves
½ teaspoon chopped coriander leaves
3 spring onions, sliced

Toss the lamb with the onion, garlic, black pepper, cumin, cayenne pepper and 1 tablespoon olive oil. Allow to marinate for as long as possible and at least an hour.

Heat the remaining olive oil in a heavy-based saucepan and cook the lamb for 2 minutes on each side. Warm the pitta breads, and cut the edges to form a pocket. Stuff the lamb into the pocket and dribble with the lemon juice, yogurt, fresh herbs and spring onions.

Per serving: 478 kcals, 23g fat, 7g saturated fat, 38g carbohydrate, 0.5g sodium

Linguine with fiery prawns
Add a little fire to your belly. The tomato sauce has a surprising kick to it that will wake up your appetite and warm your mouth.

Serves 4

3 tablespoons olive oil

2 teaspoons dried red chilli flakes or dried crushed chillies

1 teaspoon chopped thyme

400g (14oz) tinned chopped tomatoes

5 garlic cloves, finely chopped

250g (9oz) baby spinach

Freshly ground black pepper

450g (1lb) raw large prawns, shelled and split lengthways

225g (8oz) dried wholemeal linguine

2 tablespoons chopped flat parsley

Heat half the oil in a frying-pan over a medium heat. Add the chilli flakes and cook for 1 minute. Add the thyme, tomatoes and half the garlic, and stir well to combine. Cook for about 15 minutes, until the sauce has reduced and thickened. Fold in the spinach leaves and cook for 3 minutes. Season with black pepper to taste.

In a separate pan, heat the remaining oil with the remaining garlic. When the garlic begins to colour, add the prawns and cook until just pink, this should take about 2 minutes. Keep warm.

Meanwhile, cook the linguine in plenty of boiling water until *al dente*. Drain and place in a warm shallow serving dish.

Add the prawns, tomato sauce and parsley to the linguine and combine thoroughly. Serve immediately.

Per serving: 385 kcals, 11g fat, 2g saturated fat, 43g carbohydrate, 0.47g sodium

Fettuccine with purple sprouting broccoli
Purple sprouting broccoli, a springtime speciality knocks the spots off other broccoli. Broccoli is also a superveg, one of the most nutritious around. **Serves 4**

1 onion, finely diced

1 garlic clove, finely chopped

4 tinned anchovy fillets, drained, rinsed and finely chopped

2 teaspoons tinned capers, drained, rinsed and chopped

1 teaspoon rosemary leaves

1 tablespoon chopped flat parsley

1 tablespoon olive oil

350g (12oz) purple sprouting broccoli, cut into 5cm (2in) pieces

450g (1lb) fresh fettuccine

Juice of ½ lemon

Freshly ground black pepper

Parmesan cheese shavings

In a saucepan, cook the first 6 ingredients in the olive oil, until the onions have softened without colouring.

Meanwhile, boil the broccoli in plenty of boiling water for 2 minutes, add the fettuccine and cook for a further 3 minutes. When the pasta is cooked and the broccoli has broken up slightly, remove and drain.

Place the pasta and broccoli in a bowl and combine with the hot dressing. Add the lemon juice and season with black pepper to taste. Serve sprinkled with shavings of Parmesan.

Per serving: 387 kcals, 7g fat, 1g saturated fat, 68g carbohydrate, 0.22g sodium

Green pasta

The herbs and spinach provide this pasta with a little extra goodness. Quick and simple, this is also low in fat, but immensely satisfying. Great for a light lunch or dinner. Serves 6

350g (12oz) orsi or risoni
  (rice-shaped pasta)
2 tablespoons olive oil
2 garlic cloves, finely chopped
Pinch of dried chilli flakes
2 handfuls of spinach, chopped
6 spring onions, finely sliced

2 Little Gem lettuces,
  shredded
Handful flat parsley leaves,
  roughly chopped
12 basil leaves, ripped
Juice of 1 lemon

Cook the pasta in a large saucepan of boiling water, then drain and return to the saucepan.

Meanwhile, heat the olive oil in a large wok, add the garlic and chilli flakes and cook for 1 minute. Add the spinach and, using a pair of tongs, keep turning the spinach over until it has wilted, this should take about 3 minutes. Add the remaining ingredients and cook for a further 2 minutes. Season with black pepper to taste.

Add the greens to the pasta and toss to combine, then serve immediately.

Per serving: 247 kcals, 5g fat, 1g saturated fat, 45g carbohydrate, 0.02g sodium

Black olive dip

Another Mediterranean must, this is great served with raw vegetables or spread on wholegrain toast. A very moreish dip that will have keep you going until you run out of vegetables. Serves 8

225g (8oz) black olives, pitted
2 tablespoons olive oil
2 garlic cloves, finely chopped
Pinch of dried red chilli flakes
½ tsp ground black pepper

1 tablespoon tinned capers,
  drained and rinsed
Grated zest and juice of
  1 lemon
1 tablespoon chopped parsley

Blend all the ingredients in a food processor and blitz until smooth – unless you prefer to leave it slightly chunky.

Per serving: 57 kcals, 6g fat, 1g saturated fat, 1g carbohydrate, 0.68g sodium

Fiery marinated olives

Fills a 600ml (1 pint) kilner jar

350g (12oz) black and/or
  green olives, pitted, rinsed
  and dried
1 teaspoon harissa or chilli
  sauce
4 tablespoons lemon juice

1 heaped tablespoon pickled
  lemon rind, chopped
  (optional)
225ml (8fl oz) olive oil
Finely pared zest of 1 orange
  (unwaxed, if possible)
2 garlic cloves, quartered

Place all the ingredients in a non-metallic bowl and stir until well combined. Transfer to a sterilised kilner jar with a tight-fitting lid or simply leave in the bowl and cover tightly with clingfilm. Set aside for 4 days or up to 2 weeks before eating (after that the garlic could becomes rancid).

Drain the oil and lay the olives on kitchen paper to remove any excess before serving. Be warned – they are very potent.

Per 25g: 57 kcals, 6.2g fat, 0.9g saturated fat, 0g carbohydrate, 0.49g sodium

Main Courses

4

Saffron pea pilaff
A pilaff is a Middle Eastern rice dish, often cooked with meat or vegetables. In a pilaff the grains of rice should remain as separate as possible, so the rice is first rinsed thoroughly. **Serves 4**

225g (8oz) brown rice
1 tablespoon olive oil
25g (1oz) margarine
25g (1oz) flaked almonds
8 walnut halves, roughly
 chopped
25g (1oz) raisins
8 dried apricots, diced
4 cloves
2 cardamom pods

2.5cm (1in) cinnamon stick
½ teaspoon saffron strands,
 soaked in a little warm water
4 spring onions, thinly sliced
Freshly ground black pepper
1 litre (1¾ pints) vegetable or
 chicken stock
375g (13oz) podded peas
 (fresh or frozen)
3 tbs chopped coriander

Rinse the rice with cold water, then drain and set aside.

Heat the olive oil and margarine in a large heavy-based pan that has a tight-fitting lid. Add the almonds, walnuts, raisins and apricots and cook for about 5 minutes until the nuts are golden brown and the raisins are plumped up, stirring occasionally and taking care that nothing burns. Remove the fruit and nuts with a slotted spoon and set aside.

Add the cloves, cardamom pods and cinnamon stick to the pan. Cook gently for a minute or two until they become aromatic, stirring continuously. Add the drained rice to the pan and cook for 2 minutes, stirring to ensure all the rice grains are coated, then stir in the saffron mixture, the spring onions and ½ teaspoon pepper. Pour in the stock, bring to the boil, then reduce the heat, cover and simmer for 45 minutes or until the rice is fluffed up and completely tender. Add more stock as necessary, but remember it should end up quite dry.

When the pilaff has nearly finished cooking, place the peas in a pan of boiling water and simmer for 2–3 minutes until tender, then drain. Remove the pilaff from the heat and add the peas, fruit and nut mixture and the coriander. Gently fold in using a large metal spoon until well combined. Season with black pepper to taste and serve hot.

Per serving: 492 kcals, 19g fat, 3g saturated fat, 70g carbohydrate, 0.38g sodium

Pumpkin risotto with leek and yogurt
Risottos are usually quite high in fat as they are generally made with cream, butter and cheese. This version uses less cheese and low-fat yogurt. **Serves 4**

2 tablespoons olive oil
350g (12oz) pumpkin, peeled
 and cut into 2.5cm (1in) dice
2 leeks, sliced
1 tablespoon chopped sage
Freshly ground black pepper
2 onions, finely chopped
1 heaped teaspoon thyme
 leaves
1 fresh bay leaf

225g (8oz) arborio (risotto) rice
1 glass dry white wine
1 litre (1¾ pints) vegetable
 stock, boiling
25g (1oz) Parmesan cheese,
 grated
85g (3oz) low-fat Greek yogurt
2 tablespoons flat parsley,
 chopped

Heat half of the oil in a large sauté pan, add the pumpkin and cook over a fairly high heat for about 5 minutes until lightly caramelised, tossing occasionally. Reduce the heat, add the leeks and sage, and cook over a gentle heat, stirring occasionally, for another 2–3 minutes until softened but not coloured and the pumpkin is completely tender when pierced with the tip of a sharp knife. Season with black pepper, tip into a bowl and set aside.

Add the remaining oil to the pumpkin pan, then tip in the onions, thyme and bay leaf and cook for a few minutes until softened but not coloured, stirring occasionally.

Add the rice to the onion mixture and continue to cook for another minute, stirring to ensure that all the grains are well coated. Pour in the wine and allow to bubble down, stirring until it is completely absorbed.

Begin to add the boiling stock a ladle at a time, stirring frequently. Allow each addition to be almost completely absorbed before adding the next. After approximately 20 minutes, add the pumpkin mixture, the Parmesan, yogurt and parsley, and stir energetically to combine.

Season with black pepper to taste and serve immediately with a big bowl of salad leaves.

Per serving: 359 kcals, 10g fat, 3g saturated fat, 54g carbohydrate, 0.41g sodium

Smoked haddock and potato 'risotto'

Smoked food tends to be high in salt, so keep the rest of your day's salt intake as low as possible. Children, pregnant women and the elderly should not eat undercooked eggs. **Serves 2**

600ml (1 pint) semi-skimmed milk
1 onion, halved
1 fresh bay leaf
225g (8oz) undyed smoked haddock
1 garlic clove, finely chopped
2 spring onions, finely sliced
1 sprig thyme

1 tablespoon olive oil
225g (8oz) unpeeled new potatoes, diced
25g (1oz) Parmesan cheese, grated
2 tablespoons low-fat Greek yogurt
Freshly ground black pepper
2 soft poached eggs

Heat the milk in a saucepan with the onion and bay leaf. Remove from the heat and allow to infuse for 15 minute. Return to the heat. When simmering, add the fish and cook for 8 minutes. Remove the fish and set aside, then strain the cooking liquid.

Cook the garlic, spring onions and thyme in the olive oil for 5 minutes, then add the potatoes and cooking milk and cook until the potatoes are tender, this should take about 12 minutes.

Flake the smoked haddock, discarding any skin or bones and fold into the potato mix. Fold in the Parmesan and yogurt, then season with black pepper to taste.

Fill a deep pan with water and bring to the boil, the water should be at least 12cm (4 and a half inches) deep. Add 1½ tablespoons vinegar for every 1 litre of water. Crack each egg into a coffee cup and slide the egg into the water at the exact point where it has a rolling boil. After 2-3 minutes of cooking lift the eggs with a slotted spoon and lower them into iced water.

Warm through the poached eggs and place one on each warm plate. Top with the smoked haddock 'risotto'.

Per serving: 506 kcals, 22g fat, 9g saturated fat, 35g carbohydrate, 1.25g sodium

Prawn and saffron risotto

A more traditional risotto than the smoked haddock and potato version (left), this is a creamy emulsion of flavour and texture, rich and very delicious. **Serves 4**

1.2 litres (2 pints) fish stock
3 tablespoons olive oil
1 onion, finely diced
3 garlic cloves, finely diced
2 red chillies, finely diced
½ teaspoon chopped thyme
2 fresh bay leaves
375g (13oz) Arborio (risotto) rice
2 tablespoons dry vermouth

2 pinches of saffron strands, soaked in 2 tablespoons cold water
36 raw, shelled prawns
20 basil leaves, torn
2 tablespoons pesto
2 tablespoons low-fat Greek yogurt
Freshly ground black pepper

Bring the fish stock to the boil in a large saucepan and keep at a simmer.

Heat another large saucepan and add the olive oil. Stir in the onion, garlic, chillies, thyme and bay leaves, and cook until the onion is soft but without colour. Add the rice and cook for 3 minutes.

Add the vermouth and stir until the liquid is almost completely absorbed. Add the saffron with its soaking liquid and a ladle of hot fish stock. Before adding further stock, allow the liquid to be absorbed. Stir the rice frequently. Continue to add hot stock, a ladleful at a time, allowing each addition to be absorbed before you add the next. The idea is to keep the rice creamy and thick like a sauce. As you add more stock, the rice will release its starches and start to puff up. After about 20 minutes, nibble on a grain of rice to see whether it is cooked; there should still be a little bite to it.

When the risotto is ready it will have a creamy texture, with the grains of rice still separate. Add the prawns and basil, stirring as you cook for a further 2 minutes. Fold in the pesto, yogurt and seasoning. Serve immediately with a leaf salad.

Per serving: 531 kcals, 12g fat, 2g saturated fat, 78g carbohydrate, 0.64g sodium

Bay-scented salmon on roasted vegetables

Salmon is fantastic fish, full of omega-3 fats, but farmed salmon can be less flavoursome than wild. Either way, this dish provides all the taste it needs. **Serves 4**

3 small carrots, halved
2 small parsnips, halved
6 large shallots
½ small butternut squash, peeled, seeded and cut into wedges
2 garlic cloves, crushed
1 red chilli, seeded and finely chopped

1 teaspoon thyme leaves
1 tablespoon olive oil
1 teaspoon freshly ground black pepper
Olive-oil spray (see page 17)
16 fresh bay leaves
4 x 175g (6oz) salmon steaks
Juice and zest of 1 lime
3 tablespoon chopped chervil

Place half the bay leaves on a plate, top with the salmon steaks and the remaining bay leaves and season with ground black pepper. Cover with clingfilm and refrigerate for 1 hour.

Preheat the oven to 190°C/375°F/gas mark 5.

Place the carrots, parsnips, whole shallots and the squash in a pan of boiling water and blanch for 2–3 minutes, then refresh under cold running water to retain their colour.

Toss together the cooked vegetables, garlic, chilli and thyme with the olive oil and place in a preheated baking dish. Pop in the oven and roast for 45 minutes or until the vegetables are tender and golden, turning from time to time. Season with black pepper to taste.

About 10 minutes before the vegetables are ready, lightly spray a baking tray with olive oil. Place the bay leaves and the salmon on top, spray the salmon with a little oil and season with black pepper. Grill for 5 minutes on each side.

Serve the salmon on a bed of the roasted vegetables, squeeze a little lime juice over the salmon, sprinkle with the lime zest and chervil and serve with lime wedges.

Per serving: 422 kcals, 23g fat, 4g saturated fat, 17g carbohydrate, 0.1g sodium

Salmon with pea and watercress purée

Steaming is one of the best ways to cook as the food retains more nutrients, but it is perceived as boring. This should change your mind. Most of the fat here is unsaturated. **Serves 2**

Olive-oil spray (see page 17)
4 spring onions, thinly sliced
175g (6oz) podded peas (fresh or frozen)
300ml (10fl oz) vegetable stock
85g (3oz) watercress *spinach*

2 tablespoons low-fat Greek yogurt
Freshly ground black pepper
2 x 175g (6oz) salmon steaks
Lemon wedges
Steamed new potatoes, to serve

Heat a non-stick sauté pan and lightly spray with oil. Add the spring onions and cook for a few minutes until softened, stirring occasionally. Add the peas and stock to the pan, stirring to combine. Cover with a circle of greaseproof paper and allow to sweat for 2–3 minutes.

Remove the paper and add the watercress, reserving a little for the garnish, then allow to cook for a further 2 minutes or until all the liquid has evaporated. Place in a food processor with the yogurt and blend until nearly smooth – you still want a little texture. Season with black pepper to taste. Set aside.

Season the salmon fillets with black pepper and steam for 6 minutes; alternatively wrap them in foil and place in a preheated oven at 200°C/400°F/gas mark 6 for 8 minutes.

Place the salmon on the pea purée and top the lemon wedges and reserved watercress. Serve with new potatoes.

Per serving: 431 kcals, 23g fat, 5g saturated fat, 13g carbohydrate, 0.31g sodium

Baked cod with olives and spring onions

A different way of cooking white fish. Cod is a great fish because it absorbs flavours so easily. This is a flavoursome recipe, reminiscent again of the Mediterranean. **Serves 2**

1 teaspoon olive oil
2 x 175g (6oz) cod fillets
16 black olives, pitted and finely chopped
2 tablespoons chopped parsley
1 tablespoon chopped dill
1 bunch spring onions, finely chopped
2 chillies, finely diced
Juice and zest of 1 lime
Freshly ground black pepper
150ml (5fl oz) tomato juice
150ml (5fl oz) fish stock

Preheat the oven to 230°C/450°F/gas mark 8.

Lightly oil a roasting tray and place the cod in the bottom. In a bowl, combine the olives, herbs, spring onions, chillies and lime zest with the lime juice, then spread this mixture over the top of the cod.

Season with black pepper, then pour the tomato juice and fish stock around the fish. Place on the hob and bring to the boil over a medium heat.

Place the dish in the oven and cook for 12 minutes. Serve immediately, using the juices as a sauce, with a herb leaf salad.

Per serving: 209 kcals, 6g fat, 1g saturated fat, 5g carbohydrate, 0.92g sodium

Roast cod with anchovy and garlic

Another oven-cooked cod dish, but with a completely different taste. Anchovies are one of my favourite flavourings and give this recipe a completely new dimension. **Serves 4**

5 tinned anchovy fillets, drained, rinsed and roughly chopped
2 teaspoons finely chopped mint
8 garlic cloves, finely chopped
4 x 200g (7oz) cod steaks
3 tablespoons seasoned plain flour
2 tablespoons rapeseed oil
4 shallots, halved
2 celery sticks, finely sliced
1 carrot, finely sliced
2 tablespoons dry vermouth
400g (14oz) tinned chopped tomatoes
450ml (16fl oz) fish stock
3 tablespoons chopped flat parsley
Freshly ground black pepper

Preheat the oven to 200°C/400°F/gas mark 6.

Soak the anchovies in cold water for 30 minutes. Drain, then, in a food processor, blend the anchovies, with the mint and half the garlic to a smooth paste.

Make four 2.5cm (1in) incisions in each of the cod steaks and push the paste into the slits. Dust the cod all over with seasoned flour.

Heat the oil in a flameproof casserole dish. Brown the cod steaks all over, then remove and set aside.

Add the shallots, celery, carrot and remaining garlic to the same casserole dish, and cook until the vegetables start to soften. Return the cod to the pan and add the vermouth, tomatoes and fish stock and bring to the boil. Remove and place in the oven. Bake for 15 minutes, then fold in the parsley.

Season with black pepper to taste and serve in deep bowls with brown rice or new potatoes.

Per serving: 308 kcals, 8g fat, 1g saturated fat, 16g carbohydrate, 0.51g sodium

Teriyaki tuna with roast garlic noodles

Tuna lends itself to punchy flavours and this Japanese-style dish provides plenty of them. Teriyaki is a sweet-tasting sauce used to grill chicken, beef and fish. **Serves 4**

3 tablespoons reduced-salt light soy sauce
3 tablespoons mirin or dry sherry
1 tablespoons soft brown sugar
1 tablespoon grated fresh root ginger
1 bulb garlic plus 2 garlic cloves

4 tuna steaks, about 2.5cm (1in) thick
2 tablespoons olive oil
4 spring onions, finely chopped
1 teaspoon chopped thyme
275g (10oz) dried egg noodles
75g (3oz) baby spinach leaves
Freshly ground black pepper

Preheat the oven to 190°C/375°F/gas mark 5.

In a shallow dish, combine the soy sauce, mirin or dry sherry, sugar and ginger and garlic cloves. Finely chop the 2 garlic cloves and add to the dish. Add the tuna and cover. Refrigerate for 2 hours, turning from time to time.

Cut 5mm (¼in) from the top of the garlic bulb, revealing the cut edges of the garlic cloves. Drizzle with 1 teaspoon of the olive oil, wrap in foil and roast in the oven for about 30 minutes, or until the garlic is soft, then allow to cool slightly.

Squeeze the softened garlic from each clove into a frying pan, add the remaining oil, the spring onions and thyme and cook over a moderate heat until the onions are softened but not coloured.

Cook the noodles in boiling water, according to the packet instructions. Drain and tip into the garlic and onion mixture, toss to combine and fold in the spinach leaves. Toss until the spinach has wilted, and season with black pepper to taste.

Preheat the grill. Cook the tuna for 2 minutes on each side, depending on how rare you like your fish, basting with the marinade several times during cooking.

Serve immediately on the noodles.

Per serving: 573 kcals, 18g fat, 4g saturated fat, 57g carbohydrate, 0.71g sodium

Spicy fish curry

We don't eat enough fish curries and I can never understand why. This dish has beautifully balanced flavours and, unlike most curries, is relatively low in fat. **Serves 4**

700g (1½lb) fish fillets (salmon, cod or monkfish)
Olive-oil spray (see page 17)
2 onions, thinly sliced
6 garlic cloves, finely diced
½ teaspoon ground coriander
½ teaspoon ground turmeric
1 teaspoon cayenne pepper

½ teaspoon ground ginger
3 tomatoes, seeded and chopped
225g (8oz) leaf spinach, stems removed
Freshly ground black pepper
150g (5oz) low-fat Greek yogurt

Cut the fish into 2.5cm (1in) cubes.

Lightly spray a non-stick frying pan with olive oil, add the fish and fry until just cooked, this should take about 3 minutes. Remove and set aside.

Spray a little more oil on to the pan and fry the onions until they are soft but not coloured, then add the garlic and spices and cook for a further 5 minutes. Add the tomatoes and spinach and cook until the spinach has wilted. Season with black pepper, then add the yogurt. Bring to the boil and simmer for 5 minutes.

Return the fish to the sauce and heat through. Serve immediately with brown rice.

Per serving: 328 kcals, 14g fat, 3g saturated fat, 12g carbohydrate, 0.21g sodium

Spiced fish casserole

Simple one-pot dining, inspired by the West Indies. Allspice is mainly cultivated in Jamaica and is so called because it tastes like a combination of cloves, pepper, nutmeg and cinnamon. **Serves 4**

½ teaspoon freshly ground
  black pepper
8 allspice berries, crushed
4 garlic cloves, crushed
2 hot chillies, finely chopped
Juice of 2 limes
1 tablespoon olive oil
110g (4oz) monkfish
110g (4oz) haddock
4 raw large prawns, shelled

4 large diver-caught scallops,
  shucked
600ml (1 pint) fish stock
75g (3oz) French beans, cut
  into 2.5cm (1in) pieces
50g (2oz) sweetcorn niblets
50g (2oz) podded peas (fresh
  or frozen)
4 spring onions
Lime wedges, to serve

Combine the first 6 ingredients in a bowl to make a marinade. Place all the fish and shellfish in the marinade for 1 hour.

When ready to cook, add the fish and the shellfish with the marinade to the stock and bring to a rolling boil.

Add all the vegetables and cook for 4 minutes.

Serve the fish in bowls covered with the cooking liquid, accompanied by lime wedges and crusty bread.

Per serving: 153 kcals, 4g fat, 1g saturated fat, 8g carbohydrate, 0.36g sodium

Moroccan-spiced roast mackerel

Mackerel is the best-value fish on offer and has the wonderful ability to carry big flavours. It is also one of the richest sources of omega-3 fats, hence the fat content of this dish. **Serves 4**

2 tablespoons rapeseed or olive oil
2 tablespoons chopped coriander leaves
1 teaspoon chopped mint leaves
Juice of 1 lemon
½ teaspoon chilli powder
½ teaspoon paprika

2 teaspoons ground cumin
1 teaspoon ground coriander
4 garlic cloves, crushed
½ teaspoon freshly ground black pepper
4 x 350g (12oz) whole mackerel, filleted
4 tablespoons low-fat Greek yogurt

In a bowl, mix together the oil, chopped coriander leaves, mint, lemon juice, chilli powder, paprika, cumin, ground coriander, garlic and black pepper.

Place the mackerel fillets in the marinade and coat all over. Marinate for 30 minutes, turning from time to time.

Preheat the oven to 190°C/375°F/gas mark 5.

Place the fish and the marinade in a shallow baking dish, add 125ml (4fl oz) water and bring to the boil on the hob. Transfer to the oven and roast for 12–15 minutes. Remove from the oven and keep warm.

Strain the cooking juices into a saucepan and fold in the yogurt. Warm through, season with black pepper and pour over the mackerel.

Per serving: 633 kcals, 47g fat, 8g saturated fat, 4g carbohydrate, 0.18g sodium

Oatmeal herrings with tomatoes, peppers and anchovies

Most of us only try herrings as kippers, when they have been cold-smoked, but they are best when fresh. Accompany with lower-salt dishes. **Serves 4**

4 x 375g (13oz) herrings, cleaned
2 rashers lean back bacon
300ml (10fl oz) skimmed milk
150g (5oz) coarse oatmeal
Olive-oil spray (see page 17)
1 large onion, finely sliced
3 garlic cloves, finely chopped
3 tablespoons dry Martini
290g (10½oz) jar roasted red peppers and sun-dried tomatoes, drained and dried on kitchen paper

700g (1½lb) plum tomatoes, peeled and chopped
1 teaspoon chopped marjoram leaves
1 teaspoon chopped tinned capers
2 tinned anchovy fillets, drained, rinsed and chopped
16 black olives, pitted and halved

Preheat the oven to 200°C/400°F/gas mark 6.

Make 2 diagonal slashes in each side of each herring. Cut each rasher of bacon into 8 pieces and insert into the slashes in the herrings.

Dip the herrings in the milk, and then smother all over with the oatmeal.

Lightly spray a frying pan with olive oil and heat. Add the onion and garlic and cook until the onion is softened but still without colour. Add the Martini, red peppers and sun-dried tomatoes, plum tomatoes, marjoram, capers, anchovies and olives. Simmer for 10 minutes. Tip this mixture into a baking dish, big enough to accommodate the 4 herrings.

In the same frying pan, spray with a little more olive oil and pan-fry the herrings for 1 minute on each side. Remove the herrings and place on the pepper mix and bake for 20 minutes. Serve with new potatoes or a leaf salad.

Per serving: 754 kcals, 44g fat, 6g saturated fat, 44g carbohydrate, 1.34g sodium

Bouillabaisse

Entertaining in style, here are some great flavours. This is another fantastic Mediterranean recipe that traditionally contains several kinds of rock fish, saffron, onions, garlic and tomatoes. **Serves 4**

2 tablespoons olive oil

2 onions, finely chopped

4 garlic cloves, finely chopped

2 leeks, trimmed and finely chopped

1 fennel head, finely chopped, fronds reserved

400g (14oz) tin chopped tomatoes

1 teaspoon fennel seeds

1 tablespoon tomato purée

1 small bunch flat parsley, separated into leaves and stalks

2 sprigs of thyme

2 bay leaves

450g (1lb) fish bones (optional)

2 strips pared orange zest

600ml (1 pint) fish stock

500ml (18fl oz) still mineral water

½ teaspoon saffron strands, soaked in a little warm water

4 medium floury potatoes, peeled and halved

1 tablespoon Pernod

Freshly ground black pepper

1 red mullet, scaled and filleted, each fillet halved, head and bones reserved

2 x 125g (4½oz) sea bass fillets, halved

225g (8oz) monkfish fillet, cut into 4cm (1½in) chunks

450g (1lb) mussels, cleaned (about 20 in total)

6 raw large tiger prawns, shelled and deveined, shells reserved

Heat the olive oil in a large pan. Add the onions, garlic, leeks and fennel and cook gently for 10 minutes or until the vegetables are soft, but not coloured, stirring occasionally. Stir in the tomatoes, fennel seeds, tomato purée, parsley stalks, thyme and bay leaves, then add the reserved bones, if using, and the fish trimmings and prawn shells, stirring to coat. Cook for a minute or so, stirring until everything is well combined, then add the orange zest and pour in the fish stock, mineral water and saffron mixture. Bring to the boil, then reduce the heat and simmer gently, uncovered, for 30 minutes, skimming the surface occasionally to remove any froth. Strain and return to the saucepan, discarding the bones and shells.

Add the potatoes to the fish broth and cook for 15 minutes. Add the Pernod and season to taste with black pepper. Return to a simmer, then add the red mullet and the sea bass fillets with the monkfish and mussels. Bring back up to a simmer and add in the prawns. Cover and cook for another 2 minutes or until the mussels have opened and the prawns have turned pink. Using a slotted spoon, transfer the fish and shellfish to a warm serving platter and pour over the broth. Roughly chop the parsley leaves and scatter on top to serve.

Per serving: 447 kcals, 12g fat, 2g saturated fat, 35g carbohydrate, 0.58g sodium

Chicken tagine
Most people associate spicy with hot, but not so in this full-flavoured dish from Morocco. Made with either chicken or lamb, this stew is traditionally cooked over an open fire. **Serves 4**

½ tablespoon ground ginger

1 teaspoon freshly ground
black pepper

½ teaspoon ground cinnamon

½ teaspoons ground turmeric

2 teaspoons paprika

½ teaspoon cayenne pepper

8 boneless, skinless chicken
thighs, cut into 2.5cm (1in)
pieces

1 tablespoon olive oil

6 garlic cloves, crushed to a
paste

2 onions, grated

50g (2oz) dried apricots,
soaked in a little water

25g (1oz) flaked almonds

25g (1oz) sultanas or raisins

1 teaspoon liquid honey

½ teaspoon saffron strands,
soaked in a little cold water

300ml (10fl oz) tomato juice

300ml (10fl oz) chicken stock

400g (14oz) tinned chopped
tomatoes

2 tablespoons chopped
coriander leaves

Mix all the spices together. Coat the chicken with half the spice mixture and leave overnight preferably, or for a minimum of 2 hours.

In a heavy saucepan, heat the oil and brown the chicken over a high heat. Remove from the pan and set aside. Add the remaining spice mixture, the crushed garlic and grated onions to the pan. Allow the onions to soften without browning.

Add the apricots and their soaking water, the almonds, raisins or sultanas, honey, saffron and its liquid, tomato juice, chicken stock and tomatoes. Bring to the boil, reduce the heat to medium heat and cook until the sauce has thickened considerably, this should take about 20 minutes. Add the chicken and cook for a further 20 minutes.

Fold in the chopped coriander and serve immediately with the Jewelled Couscous (see page 61).

Per serving: 356 kcals, 9g fat, 1g saturated fat, 26g carbohydrate, 0.42g sodium

Chicken kebab tonnato
This is a fantastic grilled variation of a classic Italian veal dish, Vitello tonnato, which is also made with tuna and anchovies. Great for summer lunches. **Serves 2**

½ onion, finely diced

½ carrot, finely diced

½ celery stick, finely diced

2 garlic cloves, finely diced

½ teaspoon soft thyme leaves

1 bay leaf

2 tablespoons olive oil

110g (4oz) tinned tuna in
brine, drained

4 tinned anchovy fillets

150ml (5fl oz) dry white wine

150ml (5fl oz) chicken stock

300ml (10fl oz) low-fat yogurt

Pinch of salt

Freshly ground black pepper

2 x 175g (6oz) skinless chicken
breast, cut into 1.5cm (¾in)
dice

Olive-oil spray (see page 17)

Cook the onion, carrot, celery, garlic, thyme and bay leaf in the oil until the onion is soft but not brown. Add the tuna, anchovies, white wine and stock and simmer for 20 minutes or until 100ml (3½fl oz) liquid remains. Remove the bay leaf and blend in a food processor until smooth.

Allow to cool, then fold in the yogurt. Season with black pepper to taste.

Thread the chicken on to 4 satay or cocktail sticks, spray lightly with oil and grill for 3 minutes on each side. Season with a little salt and black pepper. Serve the hot kebabs with the cold tuna sauce.

Per serving: 501 kcals, 16g fat, 3g saturated fat, 15g carbohydrate, 0.94g sodium

The really useful chicken recipe

This is exactly what it says it is: a really healthy way of cooking chicken that is delicious on its own or used in salads (see Asian chicken salad, page 73), sandwiches or stew. **Serves 4**

1.5kg (3lb 5oz) free-range chicken, skin removed
4 spring onions, sliced
3 x 5mm (¼in) discs fresh root ginger
6 garlic cloves, peeled
1 chilli
10 black peppercorns

Place the chicken in a saucepan with a tightly fitting lid, cover with water and add the remaining ingredients.

Bring to the boil and simmer for 35 minutes, turning the chicken once during the cooking process. Cover with a lid and turn off the heat. Allow the chicken to relax in the liquid for 1 hour.

Remove the chicken. Allow to cool completely, then cut up and use as required.

Per serving: 212 kcals, 8g fat, 3g saturated fat, 0g carbohydrate, 0.09g sodium

Grilled chicken with coriander chutney

A very simple meal, quick to make and with lots of taste. Whenever possible, buy organic chicken as the flavour is noticeably better. **Serves 2**

Olive-oil spray (see page 17)
2 x 175g (6oz) skinless chicken breasts, skinless
175g (6oz) basmati rice, cooked

For the chutney
25g (1oz) mint leaves
25g (1oz) coriander leaves
1 small onion, roughly chopped
1.5cm (½in) fresh root ginger, peeled and grated
1 chilli, roughly chopped
½ teaspoon cumin seeds
1 garlic clove
2 teaspoons lemon juice
1 tablespoon desiccated coconut, moistened in a little water

To make the chutney, blend the ingredients in a food processor until smooth.

Lightly spray the chicken breasts with oil and cook under a hot grill for 8 minutes on each side. Serve the chicken with the chutney, basmati rice and a leaf salad.

Per serving: 546 kcals, 7g fat, 4g saturated fat, 75g carbohydrate, 0.12g sodium

Tea-smoked quail
Home smoking at its easiest: the tea, sugar and rice make a simple smoking mixture, while the Asian marinade gives fantastic flavour. It also contains much less salt than bought smoked food. **Serves 2 (4 as a starter)**

1 tablespoon sesame oil
2 tablespoons liquid honey
1 tablespoon reduced-salt soy sauce
4 quail

2 tablespoons jasmine tea leaves
2 tablespoons demerara sugar
2 tablespoons rice

Combine the sesame oil, honey and soy sauce in a bowl, rub over the quail and marinate for 1 hour.

Make a smoking mixture by combining the tea leaves, sugar and rice. Cut a circle of foil that will fit the bottom of a wok, and scrunch the sides until you have made a container about 12cm (4½in) in diameter. Place it in the bottom of the wok and put the smoking mixture in the bottom.

Place the wok over the highest heat and, once the mixture starts to smoke, place the quail on a circular metal rack that fits half-way up the wok. Cover with a tight-fitting lid and smoke for 5 minutes.

Remove the wok from the heat and allow the quail to continue to smoke without lifting the lid for 1–2 minutes.

Serve with Asian slaw (see page 73)

Per serving: 461 kcals, 29g fat, 7g saturated fat, 4g carbohydrate, 0.22g sodium

Asian pork in lettuce leaves
A lovely way of serving and eating pork. The light Oriental flavours and the fresh crunch of the lettuce leaves make this a delicious meal, hot or cold. **Serves 2**

2 garlic cloves, finely chopped
½ heaped teaspoon freshly ground black pepper
Juice and zest of 1 lime
2 tablespoons chopped coriander leaves
1 tablespoon groundnut or sunflower oil
225g (8oz) lean minced pork
1 tablespoon chopped unsalted peanuts
2 tablespoons chopped tinned bamboo shoots

1 tablespoon nam pla (Thai fish sauce) or reduced-salt light soy sauce
1 teaspoon liquid honey
1 bird's eye chilli, finely chopped
2 shallots, thinly sliced
2 large oranges, segmented
2 tablespoons chopped mint
2 Little Gem lettuces, separated into leaves

Heat a large frying pan or wok. Mix together the garlic, pepper, lime juice and zest and half of the coriander in a small bowl. Add the oil to the pan, tip in the garlic mixture and stir-fry for 30 seconds, then add the pork and stir-fry for 8–10 minutes until well browned, breaking up the mince with a wooden spoon as it cooks.

Add the peanuts, bamboo shoots, fish sauce or soy sauce, honey and chilli to the pork mixture and cook for another 5 minutes or until the liquid has almost completely evaporated, stirring occasionally. Season to taste.

Place the shallots in a bowl with the orange segments and a heaped teaspoon each of the mint and remaining coriander. Mix until well combined and pile into the middle of a large plate or platter. Stir in the remaining mint and coriander into the pork mixture and use to fill the lettuce leaves, arranging them around the orange salad.

Place a little of the orange salad on top of each pork parcel and eat immediately.

Per serving: 336 kcals, 14g fat, 3g saturated fat, 23g carbohydrate, 0.62g sodium

Brown rice bake with pancetta, greens and pecans

A really substantial meal, especially as most of the fat is unsaturated. This rice bake is great served with a leaf salad. **Serves 6**

1.5 litres (2½ pints) chicken stock	3 celery sticks, finely chopped
1 bay leaf	½ Savoy cabbage, chopped
1 sprig thyme	3 tablespoons finely chopped marjoram
225g (8oz) brown rice	½ sachet sage and onion stuffing
25g (1oz) margarine	110g (4oz) chopped pecans
115g (4oz) pancetta or lean smoked streaky bacon, roughly chopped	Freshly ground black pepper
2 onions, finely chopped	2 eggs, beaten
	Olive-oil spray (see page 17)

Bring 850ml (1½ pints) of the stock, the bay leaf and thyme to the boil. Add the rice, reduce the heat, cover and cook for 30 minutes. Transfer the rice to a large bowl, discarding the bay leaf and thyme.

Meanwhile, melt the margarine in a large saucepan, add the pancetta or bacon, onions and celery. Cook over a medium heat for 8 minutes until the onions are soft but not brown. Add the cabbage and marjoram and cook for 5 minutes, stirring regularly. Add this mixture to the rice, fold in the stuffing, pecans, plenty of black pepper and the beaten eggs.

Lightly oil a large baking dish. Fold the remaining chicken stock into the stuffing and place in the baking dish. Cover with oiled foil and bake in a hot oven for 30 minutes.

Per serving: 425 kcals, 25g fat, 4g saturated fat, 39g carbohydrate, 0.69g sodium

Bacon bollito with salsa verde

Bollito misto usually contains several meats (it means 'boiled mixed' in Italian), but this bacon version is equally delicious. It is traditionally served with salsa verde. **Serves 8**

4 small carrots, peeled and left whole	Pared rind of 1 orange, studded with 4 whole cloves
4 small onions, peeled, with root intact	12 parsley stalks
1.5kg (3lb 5oz) bacon joint, soaked overnight in water and drained	12 new salad potatoes (such as Charlotte) unpeeled
2 celery hearts, quartered through the root end	120g (4½oz) podded broad beans (fresh or frozen)
12 black peppercorns	12 baby leeks, trimmed
3 fresh bay leaves	Salsa Verde (see page 62), to serve

Put the carrots and onions into a pan large enough to hug the bacon joint and place the bacon joint on top. Add the celery, peppercorns, bay leaves and studded orange rind, then add enough water so that the liquid covers the bacon completely.

Add the parsley stalks to the pan and bring to the boil. Reduce the heat and simmer for 1 hour, skimming off any scum that rises to the top and topping up with boiling water as required to keep the bacon completely covered. Cook the bacon following the instructions on the wrapping – about 20 minutes per 450g (1lb).

Add the new potatoes 20 minutes before the end of the cooking time. Add the broad beans and leeks 10 minutes before the end. Discard the orange and parsley stalks.

Remove the bacon from the pan and place on a carving board. Snip away the string and cut away any excess fat, then carve into thick slices. Arrange the bacon slices on serving plates and spoon around a selection of the vegetables and a little broth. Serve with Salsa Verde and Dijon mustard.

Per serving: 267 kcals, 7g fat, 2g saturated fat, 12g carbohydrate, 1.39g sodium

Tuscan-style lamb
Here are more wonderful flavours from Italy. This is a really nutritious dish filled with the Mediterranean staples – tomatoes, beans, fish, olive oil and garlic. **Serves 2**

2 lamb chumps, fat and skin removed
9 tiny sprigs of rosemary
4 garlic cloves, finely chopped
Freshly ground black pepper
Olive-oil spray (see page 17)
1 onion, finely chopped
2 carrots, diced
2 celery sticks, diced
1 heaped teaspoon thyme leaves
4 tinned anchovy fillets, rinsed, drained and finely chopped
125ml (4fl oz) red wine
300ml (10fl oz) lamb or chicken stock
400g (14oz) chopped tomatoes
1 tablespoon tomato purée
400g (14oz) tinned cannellini beans, drained and rinsed
2 tablespoons chopped flat parsley

Toss the lamb chops with the rosemary and half the garlic and season with black pepper. Place in a non-metallic dish. Cover with clingfilm and leave for 1 hour at room temperature or up to 24 hours in a fridge.

Heat a sauté pan, lightly spray with olive oil and fry the onion, carrots, celery and thyme over a high heat for about 10 minutes, stirring regularly until softened and lightly browned, then stir in the remaining garlic and the anchovies.

Pour in the red wine, scraping the bottom of the pan with a wooden spoon to release any sediment, then add the stock, tomatoes and tomato purée. Season with black pepper, bring to the boil, then reduce the heat and simmer for another 15–20 minutes until well reduced and thickened, stirring occasionally.

Heat a griddle pan, barbecue or grill and cook the chumps for 5 minutes on each side until lightly charred and medium-rare. Season with black pepper.

Add the beans and most of the parsley to the tomato mixture and stir to combine. Season with black pepper and cook for 5 minutes or until heated through. Spoon into wide-rimmed bowls, garnish with the rest of the parsley and arrange the lamb chumps on top to serve.

Per serving: 606 kcals, 22g fat, 7g saturated fat, 44g carbohydrate, 0.9g sodium

Lamb kofta with spiced yogurt
The Middle East uses great spices to flavour its food and lamb absorbs them so well. The spicy meatballs and minty yogurt are an irresistible combination. **Makes 40**

75g (3oz) bulghur cracked wheat
2 tablespoons olive oil
1 chilli, finely chopped
1 medium onion, finely chopped
½ teaspoon ground coriander
½ teaspoon ground cumin
500g (1lb 2oz) leg of lamb, lean, all visible fat removed, diced
1 egg
40g (1½oz) pine kernels, finely chopped
2 tablespoons chopped mint
2 tablespoons chopped parsley

For the the spiced yogurt
2 chillies, seeded and finely chopped
1 tablespoon chopped mint
1 tablespoon snipped chives,
1 tablespoon coriander leaves, finely chopped
1 tablespoon finely chopped parsley
1 garlic clove, crushed to a paste
½ teaspoon ground cumin
250g (9oz) low-fat Greek yogurt

Soak the bulghur in cold water for 30 minutes, drain and squeeze dry.

Heat half the olive oil in a frying pan, then add the chilli, onion, ground coriander and cumin and cook over a low heat for 15 minutes. Drain, retaining the oil, and allow to cool.

Beat the egg. Place the lamb in a food processor with the egg and the onion mix and blend to a smooth paste. Remove and place in a bowl with the cracked wheat, pine kernels and herbs. Wet your hands and shape 1 teaspoon of the mixture into a small ball. Repeat to make 40 balls in total.

To make the spiced yogurt, combine all the ingredients together and leave for an hour to allow the flavours to develop.

Add the remaining oil to the reserved oil in a frying pan. Over a medium heat, fry the kofta in batches, turning regularly until brown and cooked through, this should take about 10 minutes. Keep warm in the oven. Repeat until all the kofta are cooked.

Drain the kofta on absorbent kitchen paper and serve with the spiced yogurt dip.

Per serving (4 kofta): 188 kcals, 12g fat, 4g saturated fat, 8g carbohydrate, 0.08g sodium

Shepherd's pie with a difference

Here, the cauliflower topping makes an unusual and healthier change from the traditional mashed potato. A classic English recipe.

Serves 4

Olive-oil spray (see page 17)
1 large onion, finely chopped
450g (1lb) lean minced lamb
1 tablespoon plain flour
2 bay leaves
1 teaspoon chopped thyme
1 teaspoon anchovy essence
200g (7oz) tinned chopped
    tomatoes
250ml (9fl oz) lamb, chicken or
    beef stock

2 teaspoons Worcestershire
    sauce
Freshly ground black pepper

For the topping
1 medium cauliflower, broken
    into florets
2 tablespoons low-fat Greek
    yogurt
1 egg yolk
2 tablespoons soft wholegrain
    breadcrumbs

Heat a frying pan. Spray lightly with olive oil, then tip in the onion and cook for 5 minutes until softened but not browned, stirring occasionally.

Meanwhile, heat a large, heavy-based pan and spray lightly with olive oil. Tip in half the minced lamb and cook over a fairly high heat until evenly browned, breaking up any lumps with the back of a wooden spoon and straining off any melted fat. Transfer to a plate. Cook the rest of the lamb, then return all of the lamb to the pan, adding the cooked onions and stirring to combine.

Sprinkle over the flour and then add the bay leaves, thyme and anchovy essence, stirring to combine. Add the chopped tomatoes, stock, Worcestershire sauce and a good pinch of pepper. Bring to the boil, then reduce the heat, cover and simmer for 45 minutes–1 hour until the lamb is completely tender and softened. Season with black pepper. Allow to cool, then refrigerate. Remove any solidified fat from the top.

Preheat the oven to 180°C/350°F/gas mark 4.

Meanwhile, to make the topping, place the cauliflower in a pan of boiling water, cover and simmer for 15–20 minutes or until tender. Drain and return to the pan for a couple of minutes to dry out, shaking the pan occasionally to prevent the cauliflower sticking to the bottom. Place the cauliflower in a food processor and blend until smooth. Place in a large bowl and beat in the yogurt and egg yolk. Season with black pepper to taste.

Spoon the lamb mixture into a 1.8 litre (3 pint) pie dish, discarding the bay leaves. Cover with the mashed cauliflower, then smooth over and mark with a spatula. Top with the breadcrumbs and spray with a little oil. Bake for 25–30 minutes or until bubbling and golden brown. Serve at once straight from the dish with a bowl of peas, if liked.

Per serving: 303 kcals, 13g fat, 5g saturated fat, 16g carbohydrate, 0.34g sodium

Lancashire hotpot with sweet potatoes

Another traditional dish with a twist. Sweet potatoes contain more beta-carotene than ordinary potatoes. Use water instead of stock if you want to reduce the fat and sodium. **Serves 4**

4 lamb's kidneys, skinned

8 x 110g (4oz) lamb chump chops, excess fat removed

1 heaped tablespoon plain flour

Freshly ground black pepper

½ tablespoon sunflower oil

600ml (1 pint) fresh lamb stock

Olive-oil spray (see page 17)

750g (1½lb) sweet potatoes, peeled

1 large floury potato, peeled

4 sprigs of thyme

2 onions, thinly sliced

2 fresh bay leaves

Preheat the oven to 180°C/350°F/gas mark 4.

Place the kidneys on a chopping board and cut each one in half, then, using a small pair of scissors, remove the central core and membrane. Place in a bowl with the lamb chops, add the flour and season generously with black pepper. Toss to coat, shaking off any excess.

Heat a large non-stick frying pan. Add the oil and brown the chops for 2–3 minutes on each side – you may have to do this in batches depending on the size of the pan. Transfer to a plate and set aside. Add the kidneys to the frying pan and fry for 1–2 minutes on each side, then add to the plate with the chops. Tip away any excess fat from the pan, then add a little of the stock to deglaze, scraping the bottom with a wooden spoon to remove any sediment.

Spray a heavy-based 4.5 litre (8 pint) casserole dish with a little oil. Cut the sweet potatoes into 1cm (½in) slices. Thinly slice the floury potato and set aside for the top of the hotpot. Line the bottom of the dish with half of the sweet potato slices. Place four of the chops on top, then add 2 thyme sprigs and half of the onions. Season with black pepper to taste and pop the kidneys around the sides of the casserole dish. Repeat the layers with the remaining ingredients and then pour over the stock used to deglaze the pan together with the remaining stock.

Finally, arrange an overlapping layer of the floury potato on top. Spray a little olive oil over the potato, cover and bake in the oven for 2½ hours until the lamb is completely tender, removing the lid for the final 30 minutes to allow the potatoes to go golden brown.

Serve the Lancashire hotpot straight from the casserole dish with bowls of steamed broccoli and carrots.

Per serving: 569 kcals, 18g fat, 8g saturated fat, 53g carbohydrate, 0.5g sodium

5

Desserts

Peach and blueberry gratin

So simple, so delicious, this gratin should evoke gasps of delight and anticipation from your guests. This is an elegant dessert that won't cause you too much stress to make. **Serves 4**

4 tinned peach halves in
   natural juice
75g (3oz) blueberries
50g (2oz) mascarpone cheese

175g (6oz) low-fat Greek
   yogurt
1 tablespoon caster sugar
½ teaspoon ground cinnamon

Place the peach halves in the bottom of 4 ramekin dishes and top with the blueberries.

Beat together the mascarpone and yogurt with a wooden spoon, then pour it over the fruit. Combine the sugar and cinnamon, then sprinkle over the yogurt mix.

Preheat the grill to its highest setting. Place the ramekins under the grill for 5–6 minutes until the sugar is golden. Alternatively, glaze using a cook's blow torch, chef-style. Allow to cool for a couple of minutes and serve.

Per serving: 133 kcals, 8g fat, 5g saturated fat, 12g carbohydrate, 0.05g sodium

Raspberry-ripple zabaglione

A wonderfully light and moussy custard, adorned with fresh raspberries. The slightly sharp taste of the fruit adds a little zing to this dessert. **Serves 4**

225g (8oz) raspberries
Juice of ½ lemon
2 teaspoons icing sugar
4 egg yolks
1 tablespoon caster sugar

2 tablespoons medium-dry
   sherry
2 tablespoons dry white wine
4 tablespoons low-fat Greek
   yogurt

Reserve 12 raspberries for decoration and place the rest in a food processor with a good squeeze of lemon juice. Blitz to a purée, then push through a sieve to remove the seeds. Add icing sugar to taste, leaving the fruit slightly on the tart side, then set aside.

Place the egg yolks and caster sugar in a large, heatproof bowl. Beat in the sherry and wine, using a balloon whisk. Place over a pan of simmering water and heat gently, whisking continuously until the mixture is very light but holds its shape. When it is the consistency of semi-melted ice cream, take it off the heat and continue to whisk over a bowl of iced water until cool – this prevents it from splitting.

Fold the yogurt into the mixture. Drizzle in the raspberry purée and gently swirl to create a ripple effect. Spoon into stemmed serving glasses, decorate with the reserved raspberries and serve with wafer-thin biscuits, if you like.

Per serving: 126 kcals, 6g fat, 2g saturated fat, 10g carbohydrate, 0.02g sodium

Mango fool with mango sauce

Mango and lime is a truly wonderful marriage of flavours.
This refreshing dessert is especially welcome after a heavy meal.

Serves 4

2 egg yolks

25g (1oz) caster sugar

2 tablespoons Kirsch (optional)

Juice of 2 limes

175ml (6fl oz) low-fat Greek
    yogurt

2 mangoes, peeled, stoned and
    puréed

Place a bowl over a saucepan of simmering water, add the egg yolks and sugar and beat until the mixture has thickened and trebled in volume, this should take about 10 minutes. Remove the bowl and sit it over ice. Whisk until cold, then place in the refrigerator.

When cool, add half the Kirsch (if using) and half the lime juice. In a separate bowl, whip the yogurt lightly and fold into two-thirds of the mango purée. Fold this into the egg mix. Pour into glasses or bowls and refrigerate.

Whisk the remaining Kirsch (if using), lime juice and mango purée together and pour over the mango fool to serve.

Per serving: 177 kcals, 5g fat, 2g saturated fat, 29g carbohydrate, 0.04g sodium

Poached figs with raspberries in red wine

Figs have found more favour in savoury food, but this dish will return them to their rightful puddingy place.

Serves 4

450g (1lb) ripe raspberries or blackberries
Juice of 2 lemons
Juice of 1 orange
50g (2oz) caster sugar
1 glass Zinfandel red wine
8 firm fresh figs

3 tablespoons crème de mure (blackberry liqueur) or crème de cassis (blackcurrant liqueur) (optional)
1 tablespoon freshly chopped mint
Low-fat fromage frais, to serve

Place the berries in a food processor with the lemon and orange juice and process until smooth. Strain the purée through a fine sieve into a non-reactive (not aluminium) saucepan. Discard the pips.

Add the sugar and the red wine to the berry purée and place the pan over a medium heat. Bring to the boil and simmer gently, skimming off any scum that might rise to the surface. When the sugar has dissolved, add the figs and poach for 5–6 minutes depending on their ripeness. Remove the figs to a glass bowl when cooked.

Reduce the berry cooking liquor to approximately 300ml (10fl oz). Allow to cool. Add the crème de mure or cassis, if using, and mint and pour over the figs. Cover and chill overnight. Serve with low-fat fromage frais.

Per serving: 153 kcals, 0.6g fat, 0g saturated fat, 31g carbohydrate, 0.01g sodium

Nutty apple tart with a twist

The combination of Granny Smith and Bramley apples, sweet and tart, works well here, while the cinnamon and cloves add a touch of the exotic to a classic dish. **Serves 6**

4 Granny Smith apples, peeled, halved and cored
Juice of 1 lemon
2 Bramley apples, peeled, cored and diced
50g (2oz) caster sugar
½ teaspoon ground cinnamon
½ teaspoon ground cloves

225g (8oz) ready-made short-crust pastry, thawed if frozen
25g (1oz) hazelnuts, toasted and chopped
1 egg, beaten
1 tablespoon icing sugar

Place the Granny Smith apples in a bowl with the lemon juice and pour in enough water to cover. Place the Bramley apples in a saucepan with 3 tablespoons water, cover and simmer for 20 minutes, stirring occasionally. Remove the lid and beat in the caster sugar, cinnamon and cloves until you have a smooth purée. Remove from the heat and leave to cool completely.

Roll the pastry on a lightly floured work surface to a 23cm (9in) square, then trim the edges. Transfer to a baking sheet lined with non-stick baking paper and chill for at least 30 minutes.

Drain the Granny Smith apples and slice each half into 8 thin slices.

Preheat the oven to 200°C/400°F/gas mark 6.

Remove the pastry from the fridge and spread the purée over the pastry using a spatula, leaving a 1cm (½in) border around the edges. Sprinkle on the hazelnuts, then top with the apple slices in overlapping layers. Brush the border of the pastry with the beaten egg. Bake for 15–20 minutes or until the pastry is puffed up and golden brown and the apple slices are tender and lightly golden.

Remove the tart from the oven and sprinkle over enough icing sugar to cover the apple slices. Using a cook's blow torch, caramelise the apples; alternatively place the tart under a very hot grill for a few seconds. Cut the tart into slices and serve with a little vanilla custard (see page 135), if liked.

Per serving: 308 kcals, 14g fat, 6g saturated fat, 43g carbohydrate, 0.08g sodium

Pineapple carpaccio with a fruit 'daiquiri' sauce
Thin slices of pineapple in a fruity cocktail. This dessert is as low in fat as it is high in flavour.

Serves 4

1 medium pineapple, peeled, cored and 'eyes' removed	3 tablespoons low-fat Greek yogurt
2 ripe bananas, peeled	2 tablespoons dark rum
125g (4oz) ripe strawberries, hulled	1 tablespoon honey
	4 sprigs of mint

Using a sharp knife, cut the pineapple into paper-thin slices and arrange them so they cover the base of four large plates.

In a liquidiser, blend together the bananas, strawberries (reserving 4 for decoration), yogurt, rum and honey until smooth.

Slice the 4 reserved strawberries. Drizzle the fruit sauce over the pineapple and decorate with the strawberries and mint sprigs.

Per serving: 157 kcals, 1g fat, 1g saturated fat, 32g carbohydrate, 0.02g sodium

Fruit salad with kiwi juices
Here's a fruit salad with a twist – the sweet, slightly spicy wine complements the fruits admirably. Something for the summer: light, fruity and very moreish. Serves 4

300ml (10fl oz) Gerwurztraminer wine	1 mango, peeled, stoned and diced
2 tablespoons liquid honey	10 large strawberries, hulled and halved
6 kiwi fruit, peeled	½ pineapple, peeled, cored, 'eyes' removed and cubed
2 Granny Smith apples, peeled and cored	
2 tablespoons lemon juice	

Bring the wine and honey to the boil and then allow to cool to room temperature.

In a food processor, blend 4 of the kiwi fruit with the wine and honey mix. If you don't like the seeds of kiwi fruit, pass through a fine sieve. Cut each of the remaining kiwi into 8 wedges.

Dice the apples and toss with the lemon juice. Combine with the other fruits.

Arrange the fruit salad in the centre of your bowl, ladle the kiwi juice around them, and chill until ready to eat. Serve with the kiwi wedges.

Per serving: 253 kcals, 1g fat, 0g saturated fat, 50g carbohydrate, 0.02g sodium

Fruity apple crisp
Miss your crumble? This is the next best thing. Full of fruit and spice and all things nice, the muesli or granola makes a wonderfully crispy, yet healthy topping.
Serves 6

3 Granny Smith apples, peeled, cored and each cut into 8

2 peaches, peeled, stoned and each cut into 6

50 (2oz) mixed dried fruits (cranberries, blueberries, cherries)

1 tablespoon soft brown muscovado sugar

½ teaspoon ground cinnamon

½ teaspoon apple pie spice

Juice and grated zest of 1 orange

2 tablespoons plain flour

175g (6oz) unsweetened muesli or granola

Preheat the oven to 180°C/350°F/gas mark 4.

Combine all the ingredients except the muesli or granola and spoon into a baking dish. Sprinkle with the muesli or granola and bake in the oven for about 45 minutes until golden and the fruit is bubbling. Serve with Vanilla Custard (see right).

Per serving: 203 kcals, 3g fat, 0.4g saturated fat, 43g carbohydrate, 0.02g sodium

Vanilla custard
A classic custard, this is the healthy version that you will turn to again and again. The vanilla pods give it a seductive fragrance. Serve with your favourite fruity puddings. Serves 4

2 tablespoons cornflour

4 teaspoons caster sugar

600ml (1 pint) skimmed milk

1 vanilla pod or 1 teaspoon vanilla extract

2 egg yolks

Mix the cornflour and sugar with a little milk to form a paste, then add the remaining milk.

Split the vanilla pod lengthways and, with the tip of a small knife, scrape the seeds into the milk, then pop the pods into the milk as well, or add the vanilla extract instead.

Cook the milk over a low heat until the mixture boils and thickens. Remove the vanilla pods, if using, and slowly whisk the milk into the egg yolks. Return to the heat and cook very slowly, stirring continuously until the custard coats the back of the spoon. Do not allow to boil. Serve hot or cold.

Per serving: 129 kcals, 3g fat, 1g saturated fat, 20g carbohydrate, 0.09g sodium

Fruity rice pudding
This pudding has nothing in common with school-dinner rice puddings. The real deal, full of flavour and fruit, and made with brown rice for extra fibre.

Serves 6

100g (3½oz) brown rice, washed
350ml (12fl oz) skimmed milk
4 medium eggs
25g (1oz) margarine, softened
75g (3oz) caster sugar

75g (3oz) mixed dried fruits (cranberries, cherries, blueberries, sultanas)
½ teaspoon ground cinnamon
125g (4½oz) raspberries

Bring the rice and milk to the boil in a saucepan, then reduce the heat and cook, covered, until most of the milk has evaporated into the rice, this should take about 1½ hours.

Preheat the oven to 180°C/350°F/gas mark 4.

In a bowl, beat the eggs. Fold the eggs into the rice, a little at a time, then add the margarine and the sugar.

Dust the dried fruits with cinnamon, then add them to the rice mixture.

Put a few raspberries in the bottom of 6 ramekins, then spoon the rice over the raspberries. Place the ramekins in a roasting tray and pour warm water in the tray until it reaches half-way up the sides of the ramekins. Bake in the oven for 50 minutes, and eat hot or cold.

Per serving: 248 kcals, 8g fat, 2g saturated fat, 39g carbohydrate, 0.11g sodium

Chocolate steamed pudding
Everybody loves chocolate, and this is perfect for the occasional treat. Good-quality chocolate tends to be lower in saturated fat than normal chocolate. **Serves 6**

50g (2oz) unsweetened plain cooking chocolate (minimum 70 per cent cocoa solids)
110g (4oz) plain flour
110g (4oz) caster sugar
1 tablespoon unsweetened cocoa powder

125ml (4fl oz) skimmed milk
1 egg
1 teaspoon baking powder
½ teaspoon grated nutmeg
75g (3oz) hazelnuts, toasted and chopped
Margarine, for greasing

Melt the chocolate in a bowl set over a saucepan of simmering water.

Combine the remaining ingredients, except for the hazelnuts, in a food processor or mixer and blend for 1 minute at low speed. Add the melted chocolate and blend for 1 minute at high speed. Fold in the hazelnuts.

Lightly grease a 1.2 litre (2 pint) pudding basin with margarine. Spoon the batter into the basin. Cover with a lid or a pleated greased sheet of foil tied securely with string.

Place the basin on a rack set in the bottom of a saucepan. Pour boiling water into the saucepan until it comes three-quarters the way up the side of the basin. Cook over a medium heat for about 1½ hours or until a knife or skewer inserted into the centre of the pudding comes out clean.

Remove the pudding from the saucepan and allow to cool for 10 minutes. Run a knife around the edge to loosen and invert on to a serving dish. Serve with Vanilla Custard (see page 135).

Per serving: 289 kcals, 13g fat, 3g saturated fat, 39g carbohydrate, 0.14g sodium

Bread and butter pudding with raspberry sauce

Comfort food that we all need from time to time, this is a much-beloved recipe that is worth the effort.

Serves 8

50g (2oz) sultanas

50g (2oz) raisins

4 tablespoons strong tea

1 tablespoon brandy extract or flavouring

14 slices medium-cut wholegrain bread

75g (3oz) unsalted margarine, softened

4 eggs, plus 2 egg yolks

50g (2oz) icing sugar

2 teaspoons vanilla extract

700ml (1¼ pints) skimmed milk

Pinch of grated nutmeg

2 tablespoons caster sugar

For the raspberry sauce

125g ((4½oz) fresh raspberries

1 teaspoon icing sugar

Juice of 2 limes

Place the raisins and sultanas in a small non-metallic bowl and pour over the tea and the brandy extract. Cover with clingfilm and leave to soak for at least 2 hours (overnight is best). Drain off any excess juices and reserve.

Spread the bread with the margarine. Remove the crusts and cut each slice into 4 triangles. Grease a 2.5 litre (4½ pint) shallow ovenproof dish with a little of the remaining margarine and arrange a layer of the bread triangles in the bottom of the dish, margarine-side up. Scatter over half of the soaked dried fruits and place another layer of the bread triangles on top, margarine-side up – you should have used about two-thirds of them at this stage. Set the remainder aside.

Scatter over the remaining soaked dried fruits and press down gently into the dish with a fish slice.

Whisk together the eggs, egg yolks and the icing sugar in a large jug. Add the vanilla extract and milk, whisking to combine. Pour two-thirds of this custard over the layered bread triangles and leave to stand for 45 minutes–1 hour until the bread has soaked up all of the custard.

Preheat the oven to 180°C/350°F/gas mark 4.

Pour the remaining custard mixture over the soaked bread and margarine triangles. Arrange the rest of the bread triangles on top, margarine-side up. Press the slices down firmly with a fish slice so that the custard comes half-way up the bread triangles. Sprinkle over the nutmeg and caster sugar.

Place the dish into a roasting tin and pour warm water into the tin so that it comes three-quarters of the way up the dish. Bake for 35–40 minutes or until the custard has just set and the top is golden brown.

To make the sauce, place all the ingredients in a liquidiser and process until smooth. Pass through a fine sieve to remove the pips. Refrigerate until ready to serve.

Drizzle some raspberry sauce over the pudding and serve.

Per serving: 361 kcals, 14g fat, 4g saturated fat, 49g carbohydrate, 0.47g sodium

Index

Resources

UK

Diabetes Research & Wellness Foundation
Office 101/102, Northney Marina
Hayling Island, Hampshire PO11 0NH
023 9263 7808 (Admin and Enquiries)
023 9263 6132 (Publications)
www.diabeteswellnessnet.org.uk

Diabetes UK
10 Parkway, London
NW1 7AA
020 7424 1000
Diabetes UK Careline
020 7424 1030 (voice)
020 7424 1031 (textphone)
www.diabetes.org.uk

British Dietetic Association
Charles House, Great Charles Street
Queensway, Birmingham
West Midlands B3 3HT
0121 200 8080
www.bda.uk.com

www.thinkwelltobewell.com
azmina.govindji@virgin.net
Nina.puddefoot@btinternet.com

US

Diabetes Wellness and Research Foundation
1206 Potomac Street
Washington DC 20007
DC office (toll-free)
1-877-633-3976
Helpline 1-800-941-4635
www.diabeteswellness.net

American Diabetes Association
ATTN: National Call Center
1701 North Beauregard street
Alexandria VA 22311
1-800-DIABETES (1-800-342-2383)
www.diabetes.org

CANADA

Juvenile Diabetes Research Foundation
Head Office, 7100 Woodbine Avenue
Suite 311, Markham, Ontario L3R 5J2
(905) 944-8700
Toll-free 1-877 CURE 533
www.jdrf.ca

Canadian Diabetes Association
National:
1-800 BANTING (1-800-226-8464)
Local: (416) 363-3373
www.diabetes.ca

AUSTRALIA

Diabetes Australia
GPO Box 3156, Canberra ACT 2601
Freecall helpline: 1300 136 588
www.diabetesaustralia.com.au

Acknowledgements

Writing this book has been a great pleasure for me. This was made almost effortless by the co-operation of Antony, who tirelessly took on board the sometimes challenging requests. I also have been supported by Muna Reyal, who has been understanding and obliging throughout. Special people have shaped my writing – the inspirational life coach Nina Puddefoot, dietitian and lecturer Sue Baic, my husband Shamil and my children, Shazia and Bizhan. Lastly, I would like to acknowledge the trust which the Diabetes Research and Wellness Foundation has placed in me. AG

This edition published in Canada by Whitecap Books Ltd.
For more information, contact Whitecap Books, 351 Lynn Avenue, North Vancouver, British Columbia, Canada, V7J 2C4.
www.whitecap.ca

First published in Great Britain 2003 by Kyle Cathie Limited

2 4 6 8 10 9 7 5 3 1

ISBN 1 55285 552 X

Antony Worrall Thompson and Azmina Govindji are hereby identified as the authors of this work in accordance with Section 77 of the Copyright, Designs and Patents Act 1988.

Text © 2003 Antony Worrall Thompson and Azmina Govindji
Photography © 2003 Steve Lee
Book design © 2003 Kyle Cathie Limited

Senior Editor Muna Reyal
Designer Carl Hodson
Photographer Steve Lee
Home economist Jane Suthering
Assistant to home economist Julian Biggs
Styling Penny Markham
Copyeditor Anne Newman
Recipe analysis Dr Wendy Doyle
Production Sha Huxtable

A Cataloguing In Publication record for this title is available from the British Library.

Colour reproduction by Sang Choy
Printed and bound in Singapore by Star Standard